Contents

**PART II SCIENCE FOR ALL? LESSONS FROM HOME
AND ABROAD**

List of Contributors

Alan Peacock is Lecturer in Primary Science at the School of Education, University of Exeter. He has a B.Sc. in chemistry and a doctorate in curriculum development from the University of Ulster. He taught for 11 years before moving into teacher training, first in Manchester then in Kenya. He has been researcher/evaluator in the fields of community education and INSET, and has worked for short periods in Botswana and India. His recent publications in primary science include *Science Skills* (Macmillan) and contributions to science texts for Kenya and the Caribbean.

Steve Farrow has been involved in teacher education for the past 13 years. For 10 years he was warden of a Field Studies Centre owned by an Institute of Higher Education. During this time he completed his doctorate in plant population biology. For the last three years he has been responsible for Environmental Studies, on both the Primary B.Ed. and INSET courses in the School of Education at Sunderland Polytechnic, where he is Senior Lecturer in Primary Science.

Mwangi Githui is currently Principal Lecturer in Science Education at the Kenya Institute of Education, Nairobi. He has a B.Sc. (Ed) from Nairobi University and recently gained an M.Ed. (Ed.Tech.) at the University of Wales. He was formerly Head of Science in Kamwenja Primary Teachers College, and has published several books in primary science in Kenya, as well as articles on teacher education and distance learning.

Chris Hannon is Science Curriculum Coordinator at Merrydale Junior School in Leicester. He has previously taught for 14 years in multi-ethnic schools in Leicester, and has spent the last five years as science coordinator in two primary schools, during which time he has contributed to a number of in-service courses related to science and multicultural education.

Jasbir Mann is Deputy Head at Mellor Primary School and Community Centre in Leicester. She taught in a Bradford community school after graduating, then moved to teach in Leicestershire. She spent four years at the Leicestershire Centre for Multicultural Education, first as an Advisory Teacher for English Language Support and then as an Advisory Teacher for Multicultural Education. She now works at the Leicestershire Centre for Multicultural Education as Advisory Teacher in Multicultural Education, and is producing multicultural material for teachers in maths and science.

John Meadows is Senior Lecturer in Education at South Bank Polytechnic. He holds a B.Sc. in biochemistry and an M.A. in science education, and spent 15 years teaching in primary schools before becoming an Advisory Teacher in science for ILEA. He has published several articles in *Primary Science Review*, and has recently been heavily involved with the SPACE project, investigating young children's concepts. He is currently involved in coordinating telecommunications projects between schools in London, New York and Australia.

Aldona Petrenas has a B.A. in social policy and administration in which she specialised in TESL and bilingualism. As a PGCE student at the School of Education in Leicester, she worked closely with teachers in multi-ethnic primary schools and went from there to teach infants in Sudan.

Tony Russell has been involved with primary education for 19 years, as teacher and teacher-trainer, in the UK, Botswana and Angola, where he worked with Namibian refugees. At present he is a research fellow in the APU (Science) at King's College, London. He has co-ordinated INSET courses for overseas educationists at the London Institute of Education, and has published teaching aids and articles relating to primary science curriculum development in Africa. His doctoral thesis traces the development of primary science education in Botswana.

Larry Street has recently retired after a career in primary schools and teacher training in England, East and West Africa and Hong Kong. His last post was in the Language Centre, Haringey, where he was involved in supportive group language experiments. He has recently produced materials on the Tottenham outrage, and contributed to a BBC Reading Programme.

Clare Townend is Advisory Teacher for English Language Support at the Leicestershire Centre for Multicultural Education. She has a social sciences degree and TEFL qualifications, and has been a primary teacher in Leicester for five years. She has contributed to earlier publications on science in a multicultural society.

Barry Troyna is Lecturer in the Social Aspects of Education at the University of Warwick. He has also taught and carried out research on antiracist education at the Universities of Leicester and Aston, Sunderland Polytechnic and, in 1987, Monash University in Melbourne. Amongst his recent publications are *Racism, Education and the State* (Croom Helm) which he wrote with Jenny Williams, *Racial Inequality in Education* (Tavistock) and *Children and Controversial Issues* (Falmer), edited with Bruce Carrington. His new book on antiracist education, written with Bruce Carrington, is published by Routledge.

Mike Watts is currently Senior Lecturer in Science Education at Roehampton Institute. He gained his doctorate for work within the study of children's conceptualisation of parts of physics, and is a fellow of the College of Preceptors. He has taught for many years in an inner-city comprehensive in Hackney, London and in Kingston, Jamaica. His research has concerned many aspects of children's learning in science, and curriculum development in schools. For over three years he worked as part of the central team of the Secondary Science Curriculum Review. he has published widely in science education – most recently on teaching and learning in science classrooms, coursework for GCSE and a series of INSET workshop packs on equal opportunities, gender and race. He has contributed a number of articles and conference papers on multicultural and antiracist science.

Barbara Wyvill has been warden/director of both the ILEA's North London Science Centre and Science Teachers Centre South. She obtained a B.Ed. in 1974 and an M.Sc. in entomology in 1978. Her career has included teaching in multiracial schools, both primary and secondary, and directing the JISTT project, during which she wrote the ILEA primary science guidelines, *Helping Children to Become Scientific*. She has also worked for short periods in Kenya, India and Indonesia.

Introduction

Alan Peacock

The tale of why a book was written is not always worth the telling; but in this case, it reveals so much about the book's subject matter that I decided it was worth relating. It began almost by accident. In 1986, I was asked to put on a short course for teachers at the School of Education in Leicester where I then worked: the work was to have some form of multicultural dimension, but otherwise I had a free hand. I decided to link it to my main teaching commitment, which was with the Primary PGCE Science course, and decided to call the course 'Multicultural Science in Primary Schools', thereby hoping to attract both teachers and trainees onto the course.

My next step, being relatively new to Leicester at the time, was to look around for 'experts' in this field. I got in touch with all the obvious agencies, and came into contact with primary science specialists who claimed to know little about multicultural education, multiculturalists who knew about science in secondary schools, but nobody who admitted to any expertise in both primary science and multicultural education. I then searched the literature, and came to the same conclusion, namely that science and multicultural education rarely met, and when they did, it was almost always in relation to the secondary phase of education. I first imagined that I would have to become an 'expert' myself, if I wanted to run the course; then on reflection, I decided that a better strategy might be to act as an agent in bringing together people with expertise and interest in one or other dimension, in order that we could learn from each other.

The first short course was thus developed by Jasbir Mann, Clare Townend and myself, combining our knowledge of multicultural education, language support teaching and primary science. The teachers and students on the course, from a range of different backgrounds, provided another range of expertise and knowledge, and we began to map out what the needs of teachers in this field might be. Two urgent requirements proved to be (i) the need to produce materials reflecting cultural diversity, and (ii) the need for background information to give confidence to teachers, particularly those working in all-white schools. The first of these needs we tackled through a series of workshops at which teachers tried out ideas on each other, developed materials and subsequently reported back on their use in the classroom. Some of this work is reported below, particularly in Chapters 2 and 3.

The second need clearly required somebody to compile a book; I still didn't believe that such a book had yet to be written (and even now, I'm sure somebody else must be doing what I'm doing!) but having re-checked the library catalogue, I decided it was time to take the bull by the horns and invite all the people who might have a useful contribution to make, to offer a chapter.

The responses surprised me in two ways. I was taken aback by the enthusiasm for the idea of a book on the subject; but at the same time, I was astonished at how many experts in their field felt that, like the people in Leicester I had contacted, they did not have the combination of expertise that the book required. Thus this book is not a compilation of the thoughts of experts in 'multicultural science in primary schools' because such expertise is a very rare commodity, perhaps exemplified best by Barbara Wyvill's opening chapter. Instead, it brings together a number of different perspectives on the question of how teachers can best build a multicultural/antiracist dimension into their teaching of science at the primary level, and what are the implications of attempting to do this. These perspectives include those of the trainee teacher, class teacher, advisory teacher, teacher trainer and researcher: those with expertise in primary science, multicultural/antiracist education and language support; and those of the majority culture in Britain, ethnic minority groups and colleagues in developing countries.

The two parts of the book therefore look at two major concerns from a number of angles. The first concern, taken up in Part I, is with the 'how to' questions that classroom teachers often ask in attempting to make a start in this area. Questions such as, What topics and ideas are useful for developing multicultural science? How can we make sure we acknowledge the cultural diversity of the school and the wider community? How can we make science and science materials accessible to children whose mother tongue is not English? How do we tackle these topics in all-white schools? How to incorporate a multicultural dimension within the constraints of the National Curriculum? What kinds of resources and INSET support are available?

The second major concern, dealt with in Part II, is with the underlying rationale for a multicultural approach to primary science. 'Science for all' has been the accepted doctrine since Swann and the 1985 Policy Document on Science: but what does this mean in practice? Do we really mean *all*, and if so, are we prepared for the implications? These are carefully spelled out by Barry Troyna and Steve Farrow. But the omissions from policy statements are as revealing as their contents, and Mike Watts has pursued these through to the most recent National Curriculum documents, in order to highlight what policy statements might say, if they were to reflect the kinds of good practice delineated by the chapters of Part I. Finally, Tony Russell and Mwangi Githui look at primary science from the perspectives of other cultures, and by so doing, expose some of the contradictions and unquestioned assumptions we make about the scientific process, science knowledge and their place in the growth and development of children. They remind us forcibly of the fact that we have a great deal to learn about people as well as about science.

But back to the tale of the book. While we were running our programme of workshops in Leicester, one particular question concerned us more than all the others, and it was this. Why, when both primary science and multicultural education have received such prominence in recent years, has so little attention been paid to what we might call, in shorthand, 'multicultural primary science'? Why, for example, did articles in the primary journals about 'science with fruits' or 'windmills' or whatever, almost always ignore opportunities to use examples from a range of cultures? We were not content to stop at the 'why' of this, either; we wanted to work out what positive steps could be taken to do something about it. I hope, therefore, that the remainder of this book succeeds in illuminating the reasons why, but even more, I hope that readers will find in every chapter something which positively encourages them not only to see primary science differently, but also to act in order to make 'multicultural science for all' a reality.

What are the reasons, then, why so little attention has been paid to this field? A key point made by Barry Troyna and Steve Farrow is that, despite the growth of primary science and the stress on multiculturalism, the two sectors of the teaching profession which have shown greatest reluctance to acknowledge a multicultural dimension in their work have been primary teachers and science specialists. And the roots of this reluctance may have many origins.

In the case of primary teachers, for example, the notion of multicultural science suggests a double insecurity. The benefits of 'learning with' children, so well demonstrated in Chris Hannon's chapter, may for many teachers be outweighed by fears of revealing their ignorance of science on the one hand, and fears of offending the cultural norms and beliefs of the children on the other. Others have pointed to the intimidating language and terminology of science, and its negative connotations for women teachers in particular: this is bound to be compounded when teachers are attempting to deal with science concepts in what for children is their second language. As yet, few mother tongue publications exist in science for young children; even in a country as large as India, for example, primary school science texts are centrally published in English, and it is left to individual states or regions to create their own vernacular language versions.

Shortage and availability of suitable resources is thus a major demotivating factor for many primary teachers, and Chapters 3, 4 and 5 attempt to offer help with this problem. But resourcing is not the end of the story: as Mike Watts and Tony Russell both point out, there are also difficulties with perception of the nature of science. Teachers in primary schools in Britain are likely to adopt the dominant world outlook that sees science as what white, western scientists do: the view that science has always been 'out there' waiting to be discovered, and is hence no different, whatever culture you belong to. Water always flows downhill, crops always die without water . . . where's the multicultural dimension? It is a question that has to be answered, and it is answered in Part II of this book by several authors who demonstrate, in various ways, that science is as dependent on culture as art, music or poetry. For example, some of the most important scientific principles are defined in metaphorical language: forces 'act', magnetic poles 'attract' or 'repel', species 'adapt'. Such language is clearly culture-bound, and not independent of human temperament and ways of seeing. Likewise school science, therefore; since it is defined by society, as Mike Watts shows, why cannot it be re-defined to reflect the multicultural nature of society?

Another possible reason for teachers retreating from involvement with multicultural science is the inescapable political dimension. Barry Troyna and Steve Farrow point out starkly what equal access to science for all must mean, and there are no doubt many teachers who are as yet intimidated by this prospect of democratised relationships, particularly when the National Curriculum documents continue to skate perfunctorily around the issue. But on the positive side, the authors also suggest how this vagueness itself can be a benefit, in allowing teachers space to explore appropriate ways of working, and thus to dig out understanding of how they can overcome obstacles.

A final factor behind the lack of practical involvement in multicultural science is perhaps the nature of the current pressure on primary teachers. As I have suggested elsewhere (Peacock, 1989) parental perceptions of science in the primary phase are still quite vague, and often at odds with the requirements of the National Curriculum. Hence there is as yet no effective pressure of demand from parents to work in the ways described in the first half of this book. At the same time, immense demands are currently being made as a consequence of the Education Reform Act, both from the National Curriculum requirements and local management of schools, and ultimately all these demands put pressure on teachers, who inevitably respond to the most urgent issues of the moment, of which multicultural education is not one. On the contrary, many people are concerned at the moment that primary schools will respond to these pressures by placing an increased attention on teaching and assessing factual knowledge, particularly in science, as a way of ensuring that their children reach higher levels of attainment.

But even if this turns out to be the case, it provides ways in to multicultural teaching. For example, teachers are likely to be anxious about Attainment Target 4, and the need to teach about similarities and differences between children. This provides a focus for in-service training, which can then address the wider issues of multicultural science, as John Meadows has suggested in Chapter 6. One key point stressed in this chapter is that even the youngest children bring to school culturally determined perceptions about scientific phenomena, as well as positive attitudes to investigative work. Therefore it is essential to respect their thinking and attitudes, whatever these might be, and to build on their strong motivation to find out about and make sense of the world around them.

What I hope this book says, therefore, is that whilst it is easy to be pessimistic about the current situation in relation to teaching science in a genuinely multicultural, never mind antiracist way, nevertheless there are many things which can be done by teachers which can bring about positive changes, and I will conclude this introduction by suggesting what some of these might be.

The first point, which cannot be overemphasised, is that children of all backgrounds and cultures find science fun, which makes it so much easier for teachers to try new ideas and take risks. Secondly, various chapters of this book have stressed the considerable overlap between the principles underlying antiracist education, language development and the processes of science. Observing, interpreting evidence, describing, communicating, sharing ideas and collaborating to achieve progress are part of all these, and can therefore be used to reinforce each other in the ways described in detail below. This common ground is a powerful platform for teacher and pupil development.

One spin-off of this which has already been touched on is the opportunity it provides for teachers to learn alongside, even to learn from, their children. Jasbir Mann shows us how much teachers value this kind of classroom-based in-service work with their own children and colleagues, and it is happily a form of INSET provision which is increasingly being fostered by local authorities. A further opportunity, particularly in multi-ethnic classrooms, is the way in which children can use the process of investigative science to support and teach each other, as Aldona Petrenas and Larry Street have shown in their examples of children using science as a vehicle for language learning. And it is here that recognising and celebrating cultural differences is of great value to the developing understandings of children and teachers alike.

What positive encouragement can be given in relation to the provision of resources, when schools are faced with the prospect of even less money to spend? The first point to stress is that resources are everywhere, but often in unexpected (in other words non-scientific) places! Chris Hannon and Jasbir Mann obtained all they required from the local shops and children's own homes: but then, you might say, they were living in a multi-ethnic community. On the other hand, we all have equal access to large supermarkets and the national media, and much of what they provide is increasingly multi-ethnic. One example is the BBC's publication *Instruments of the World* (BBC Enterprises, 1988), published to accompany a schools music series on radio, but which has enough multicultural science and technology in it to keep most schools going for a long time. And I have found that in Devon, where I now work, there are very few multicultural necessities which I can't buy that I could in Leicester, including the delicious karelas that Chris Hannon's children had so much fun investigating.

Another major opportunity, although it may not as yet appear to be such, is the requirement of assessment within the National Curriculum. Mwangi Githui has demonstrated the power of assessment to influence the way teachers teach, and the way parents value what children learn. Changes in the kind of tests given to children probably exert more influence on teaching and learning than any other curriculum change. Certainly, such changes can be a positive or negative influence; but we should not at this stage assume that change is bound to be negative. I know from my own experience as a teacher trainer in Kenya how new types of test question succeeded in discriminating in favour of, for example, rural and nomadic children, who previously had been at a major disadvantage in comparison to urban children in the primary leaving examination. There is no reason in principle, therefore, why the same cannot happen here. But it needs teachers to care about and devise the kinds of assessment which are equally appropriate to all children, whatever their cultural background.

Along with the development of assessment techniques and the public reporting of results is bound to come an increased parental concern for what is being taught and how, and this too could soon begin to prompt schools to be more responsive, particularly as local management also begins to take effect. As already pointed out, parental knowledge about science in primary schools is still probably too vague to influence opinion: but once test results begin to be published, parents will want to know more, and to have a say in the way science is dealt with. Many schools are already beginning to have parents' evenings at which mothers and fathers get 'hands on' experience of science activities, or are putting on exhibitions of childrens' work in science. Under such public scrutiny, I believe, schools will want to ensure that their approach to science reflects the real concerns of their community.

For underlying all these optimistic assumptions – and each year as a new generation of trainees goes out to join the profession, my optimism is renewed – is one crucial factor which is emphasised by Barry Troyna and Steve Farrow: namely that despite the changes being made in our system, the pressures on teachers and the demoralisation which goes with it, the notion of equality of educational opportunity is still a fundamental tenet which no government, local authority or board of governors is going to gainsay. I therefore leave the last word of this introduction to them:

Given then, that so many of the principles by which Science is most effectively learned in primary schools are also those of antiracist education, surely primary science has no excuse for not being in the vanguard of multicultural/antiracist practice?

PART I

MULTICULTURAL SCIENCE IN PRACTICE

Chapter 1

Classroom Ideas for Antiracism through Science in Primary Education

Barbara Wyvill

Introduction

Slowly the parachute descended, depositing Mrs Shah safely onto the floor. 'Three whole seconds that time!' announced Roulla as she stooped to pick up the little doll. Meanwhile Kathleen, Tom, Wayne and Aziza were planning a fair test to show whether their paper darts were improved when a small mass was attached. On the other side of the classroom Hsiao-chin was showing her group how to make a kite before they could go on to find out why it needed such a long tail. Sean and Darren were busily occupied on the carpet in the book corner, surrounded by books on air and flight. They appeared to be cutting pictures from magazines and sticking them into some of the books – with relish. By the window, Samina was quietly watering an unusual looking plant. Ms Abbott, the children's teacher, was occupied with another group of children who were discussing the effects that aeroplanes had on their lives. There was certainly a lot of science going on in this classroom. Was any of it antiracist?

At the beginning of the year Ms Abbott asked all the children in her class to draw a picture of a scientist doing something. Not surprisingly, the majority of the pictures were of white, middle-aged to old, white-coated, male scientists. She used the opportunity to discuss with the children why so few of their scientists were women, none of them black or Asian and none of them young. She found that few children in the class could name a woman scientist (apart from Marie Curie) and none knew of any black scientists. Resolving to tackle these problems later in the term she set about asking the children to describe what their scientists were doing. Here she found less conformity. Most of the scientists in the children's pictures were actively engaged in experimenting, discovering, finding out, solving problems or looking at things through microscopes.

They were engaged in process science. A few of the scientists were described as evil and were planning ways of destroying the earth while one was looking for a cure for cancer and another was turning lead into gold. So between them the children had appreciated that science has social, political, economic and moral dimensions.

Antiracist science in the classroom begins by defining science as

(i)   an activity carried out by people
(ii) an activity which has relevance to all aspects of human life
(iii) an activity which involves processes of thought and discovery.

If science is defined as something that everyone can do and as something that is relevant to everyone, then children can learn to become scientific regardless of their class, gender, special needs or ethnic origins. This view of science differs from the traditional idea that school science is concerned only with understanding and learning a collection of facts and ideas. Instead it defines a set of processes through which children (and other people) can investigate themselves and the world around them. Different authors on process-based science vary in the exact list of scientific processes (or process skills) which they describe, but the following are ones that are generally agreed to be essential: observing; asking questions; making hypotheses; planning and carrying out experiments; interpreting; recording; presenting. It is through carrying out practical scientific activities involving these processes, discussing their findings and reflecting on them, that children build up scientific concepts and ideas.

In Ms Abbott's classroom science was not the only 'subject' that the children were learning. Roulla was measuring time – mathematics, Hsiao-chin and her group were kite-making – CDT, Ms Abbott's group were discussing – language. The children were experiencing science as an integral part of the curriculum. This is important, so that science is seen not as a separate entity but as part of their whole experience. If science is to be learnt as an integral part of children's lives, it should start from things that interest them. Things that are of interest and concern to children often derive from their own culture. For example, Hsiao-chin brought to school a type of kite that her mother had learned to make in Hong Kong and which her mother had helped her make at home. She then volunteered to show the other children how to make one too, before beginning their investigations.

In Ms Abbott's classroom most of the children work together in groups. Their teacher encourages them to collaborate because in this way the children learn to co-operate with each other and they are able to share experiences and tasks. Although they work largely in friendship groups, Ms Abbott ensures that children usually work in mixed groups.

Children can learn to be antiracist through practical scientific activities integrated within the whole primary curriculum and set within a social, political, economic and moral framework. Antiracist ideas are further fostered if the children work together on material that is relevant to their lives. In the following sections, practical examples of antiracist science teaching will be examined, as they arise in typical classroom topics.

HELP CHILDREN TO BECOME ANTIRACIST AS THEY BECOME SCIENTIFIC

- Challenge stereotypes of scientists.
- Encourage children to find out about non-western scientists.
- Teach a process-based approach to science.
- Encourage all children to work together in groups.
- Integrate science with the rest of the curriculum.
- Start from children's interests.
- Teach science in a social, economic, political and moral context.

Multicultural resources

Process-based science requires children to learn through handling materials and gaining first-hand experience as they carry out practical activities. The material resources needed for science are many and varied. However, only a few of these materials are designed specifically for scientific activities while the majority are everyday objects or are things that are commonly used in primary classrooms. Often scientific activities form part of an integrated topic. The resources used for the topic work are commonly selected by teachers, less often by children. When choosing resources for science a teacher can take into account the culture of the children (s)he is teaching and other cultures in Britain and the rest of the world. It is important that teachers do this so that children learn that objects common in their own culture are recognised and valued. In addition, other children learn to recognise and value things from cultures which are not their own. This sharing can only enrich everyone's experience.

Often, this multicultural approach to resources in science is labelled 'tokenist'. This can be true if it is the only antiracist strategy used but not if it forms part of a wider policy on antiracism. Some ideas for using multicultural examples are described below.

Food

The two commonest topics where a multicultural use of resources is made are 'Food' and 'Growing plants'. A topic on 'Food' might contain some work on bread because people from many cultures eat some form of bread. Children can begin by observing different types of bread – pitta, cholla, rye bread, chapattis and sliced white. They can look at it unaided or with the help of a hand lens or a microscope. They can feel it, smell it and taste it. Observing differences such as the amount of holes in the different types may lead them to ask questions such as: 'How did the holes get there?' or 'Why does the number of holes vary?' These questions could lead on to children examining recipes and testing hypotheses concerning the way holes get into bread. Having perhaps tried out some of the recipes they may go on to make up their own recipe for a type of bread not in their cookery book. A project such as this could be initiated by a teacher asking the children to bring in a piece of the bread that they usually eat at home.

Many large supermarkets carry a huge selection of fresh fruits and vegetables. These days, an enormous variety of foods from all over the world can be purchased even from smaller shops, especially in larger towns and cities.

Fruit and vegetables can be the starting point for many investigations. One starting point is for children to observe various fruits and vegetables and then to discuss what part of the plant they come from. Predictions can be made about what is inside fruits and vegetables before cutting them to find out. (This kind of work is described in more detail in Chapters 2 and 5.)

Plants

Seeds from 'exotic' fruits can be planted and grown. There are several books that give help with doing this. Various beans (not red kidney) and seeds can be used for experiments to find out, for example, the best conditions for growth. This can be done at low cost if children are asked to bring in the seeds left from fruits they have eaten at home. Other parts of plants may also grow. Sugar cane, for example, will grow if it is green, is cut just below a node, planted in potting compost and watered regularly. In fact, any experiment that is normally carried out using common British-grown fruits and vegetables can be done with 'multicultural' food plants. In, addition plants which are not fruit plants but which have an economic importance can be used for growth experiments.

Music

Sound and music are good starting points for scientific activities. Often such a topic will start with children exploring the different ways in which they can produce sounds from musical instruments. Such a collection of musical instruments can include not only those usually found in schools but instruments from all over the world. However, some musical instruments are expensive to buy so perhaps they can be borrowed from the LEA advisory service or from a local secondary school. Less expensive musical instruments include: pipes and flutes from various parts of the world – Africa, South America, Ireland; small African and Asian drums; castanets from Spain and maracas from South America. Few stringed instruments are cheap to buy, but they are fun to improvise.

Recently, I worked with a group of nine and ten-year-old children from Camelot Primary School in London. We started by discussing sound and what different aspects of sound they could perceive with their ears. Following this I presented them with a selection of musical instruments from all over the world and asked them to investigate, first, the different methods of producing sound and, secondly, the ways in which different notes could be produced on each instrument. The children were very interested in the instruments and wanted to know their names and where they came from. They particularly liked playing the sansa harp (ordered from the Oxfam catalogue) and an un-named stringed instrument I had found in Kenya. They compared the African and South American wind instruments with the recorders that they played themselves and were very pleased with themselves when they managed to get a note out of the wooden flutes. After a while they decided to put the instruments into sets. They divided them into four groups: instruments with strings which you pluck; those which you beat; those which you blow; and those which you shake. Some lively discussion resulted when they found some instruments which could be played in more than one way.

Afterwards the children discussed the ways in which the pitch and loudness of notes could be altered. They noticed a pattern: that the longer the wind instrument or the more holes covered the deeper the note. They also observed that longer strings made deeper notes. This led them to make two hypotheses: the longer the pipe the deeper the note; and the longer the string the deeper the note. We then discussed ways of testing these hypotheses. I showed them how to make sounds from straws by cutting one end into a blunt point, putting that end into the mouth and blowing. At first they found it difficult to make a sound but before long everyone was successful. Two of the children made about a dozen of these pipes in different lengths so that they could test out the first hypothesis. Three others used rubber bands to test out the second one. This group did not have time to get very far but the children soon realised that the thickness of the bands and the tension which they were under made differences which they wanted to explore. Meanwhile two more of the children experimented with making an instrument out of bottles by putting varying amounts of water in them and then striking them with a beater.

I would have liked to have had more time with these children so that they could have continued their explorations and perhaps have investigated sound as a vibration. One way of demonstrating that sound is a vibration is to make a small drum by stretching a sheet of polythene over an empty baked bean tin with both ends taken off. The polythene is secured with a rubber band.

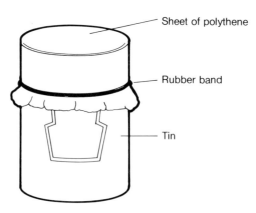

Sheet of polythene

Rubber band

Tin

If sugar grains are put on the drum skin and the open end of the tin is placed over the speaker of a tape recorder, the grains dance when it is switched on. A tape is needed, of course, and this could be music from any part of the world. Another way of showing that sound is a vibration is to strike a tuning fork and touch the surface of some water with one of the prongs and see what happens.

One piece of problem-solving that children (and teachers) enjoy is to make their own musical instruments. To do this they need to use the experiences which they have gained through investigating ready-made instruments; through experimenting with pitch and loudness; through exploring the range of materials used in construction; and through exploring the nature of sound. A valuable resource to me is *Instruments of the World* (BBC, 1988). As a final activity, composing musical stories using both the home-made and other musical instruments can be great fun. The stories can either be made up ones or stories from the children's own cultures.

I learnt how to play Jingle Bells with bottles that are emptied and filled up with water. They had different amounts of water in them so when you tap them with a rubber beater they make different sounds. I tried to work out Jingle Bells. When I did it I gave Barbara my version and she gave me hers. They were slightly different. We decided that my version was more like the original version. So I learnt it. I took a lot of hard work but I did it in the end. Most of all, I enjoyed it.

Written By victoria Barbary (age 9)

Festivals and celebrations

People from all over the world have festivals and celebrations – birthdays, saints' days, religious festivals, festivals to celebrate the seasons, national holidays and so on. In the UK some celebrations are shared by several groups of people and some are culturally specific. The origins and rituals of various festivals may be explored through the religious and historical parts of the curriculum. Science, too, can add to their fuller understanding.

Many different religious festivals have water and light as important themes in their rituals. 'Science from candles' and 'Water' are topics that are rich in scientific experiences. While this may be labelled 'multiculturalism', through this type of work children can learn about similarities between various festivals and can also learn to understand, appreciate and value each others' celebrations.

Here are a few examples of practical work with candles and with water and one idea of how to combine the two!

CANDLES

Start by observing a candle. How many observations can the children make about an unlit candle and a lit one (NB: safety)? How do younger children explain the melting wax? Try making candles (NB: safety). What are the optimum conditions for candle-making? How long do they take to set? How can this be speeded up? How can you vary the pattern of colours in a candle? (See for example the book on *Candles*, in the Teaching Primary Science Series published by Macdonald Educational (Bird and Diamond, 1975).)

WATER

There are thousands of things to do with 'Floating and sinking' – primary teachers are only too familiar with these. Here are some suggestions for other lines of enquiry. Why is water important in our lives? What happens in areas where there is too much or too little water? Irrigation is important; can you devise a method of making water go uphill? Design an experiment to show how soil erosion from a hillside can be retarded, or ways in which dirty water can be made clean. (See Chapter 5 for resources on water.)

CANDLES AND WATER

Here is a problem to solve – make a candle burn under water!

HELP CHILDREN TO BECOME ANTIRACIST AS THEY BECOME SCIENTIFIC
- Use artefacts, plants and foods from other cultures for scientific investigations.
- Encourage children to bring in objects with which they are familiar.
- Select dolls from a variety of cultures for use in scientific activities.
- Play music from different parts of the world when it is incidental to scientific activities.
- Value other people's customs and teach children to do the same.
- Let festivals and celebrations be a starting point for scientific activities.
- Enjoy all festivals and celebrations wherever they come from.

Incidental resources

Some of the resources that are used in science are only incidental to the actual investigation but these too can reflect multicultural diversity. Dolls have various functions in primary classrooms. In the introduction to this chapter, Roulla was using a small Asian doll for lowering by the parachute that she and her friends had made. The doll was part of a set of eight: two parents, two grandparents, a boy and a girl and two baby dolls. African, European and Chinese sets can also be bought. In another problem children may be asked, for instance, to find out which fabric is best for making a raincoat for an African doll, or a hat for a Russian doll, etc.

Ideas of race: similarity and continuous variation

What is 'race'? When groups of teachers have been asked the question 'What race are you?' they answered: 'British'; 'I'm Black'; 'English'; 'My mother is Irish and my father is Chinese'; 'Caucasian'; 'I'm a McDonald'; 'Asian'; 'I belong to the human race' and so on. Each has interpreted the meaning of 'race' in a different way. The Shorter Oxford English Dictionary defines 'race' as 'a group of persons, animals or plants, connected by common descent or origin'. Each of the teachers' statements about themselves, although different, incorporates this idea of descent or origin.

'Race' cannot be regarded as a scientific term since it is far too imprecise. Examining the teachers' statements shows that they regard race variously as: nationality, state or continent of origin, family, colour or species. They were not using 'race' in a scientific way. The Shorter Oxford English Dictionary also gives this definition of race: 'a group of persons, animals or things, having some common feature or features'. Some biological textbooks (especially older ones) often divide the human race into distinct races – Caucasian, Aryan, Mongoloid, Negroid, etc., as though there were a clear distinction between them, often characterised by a distinct set of physical characteristics. This physical stereotyping is often coupled to erroneous and harmful behavioural stereotyping of certain groups. Everyone has heard racist jokes in which various groups are labelled as mean with money, lazy or stupid.

So what can a teacher do to change people's ideas about the pseudo-scientific concept of race? Human beings all belong to the same species. As members of the same species, we have a great many characteristics in common. This is something that can be stressed in the classroom. 'Ourselves' is a topic that frequently occurs in primary schools. Often it includes divisive activities such as: making bar charts to show the distribution of eye colour within the class; testing to see who has the strongest hair; finding ways of measuring hand size, foot size, head size and then making comparisons between children. All of these only serve to remind children of individual differences, a process which can be distressing to the smallest and largest, the fattest and thinnest or the darkest and lightest children in the class.

A far better approach is to require children to begin by looking for similarities amongst individuals. If you ask children in what ways we are alike they usually answer in terms of physical characteristics: 'We have two eyes, a nose, a mouth, hair, two legs, etc.' With some encouragement they will also suggest that we are alike in our abilities (we can all sing, see, walk, learn, love, make mistakes, grow, eat . . .).

But of course there are differences between individuals. Children are observant and will notice these. Take skin colour for example. We are alike in that we all have skin. Skin serves the same functions for all of us. Everyone's skin is made up of cells, has sweat glands and hairs and (except for albinos) contains the pigment melanin. But here the differences begin. Melanin may be spread evenly or occur as freckles in some people. Skin colour varies from very pale to dark. There is variation. Variation can be found within any species and gives the potential of evolutionary advantage to a population in a changing environment. Variation in skin colour is an example of continuous variation as all skin colours can be shown to grade one into another. The reason for this continuous graduation is because differences in skin colour are caused largely by the quantity of melanin in the skin. (Other factors which affect skin colour are the thickness of the skin and the degree to which the blood capillaries of the skin are temporarily dilated.)

Now, the advantage of looking at continuous variation is that if it can be shown that each set of characteristics can be placed on a continuum, then the idea of race (as a group of people having a set of fixed characteristics) can be shown to be false. Most teachers who have asked children to paint pictures of themselves will be familiar with the lurid colours they use to paint their faces. Often, too, black children will paint themselves pink or white. But if children are asked to mix a paint colour as close as possible to their own skin colour, they must first of all observe their skin closely then solve the problem of paint mixing and matching. Given red, blue, yellow, black and white paints this can always be done. The children may be surprised to find out that all skin colours can be matched by using different proportions of the same paint. 'White' children may be surprised to see how unwhite they are! If each child uses her/his mixed colour to paint a small piece of paper then it will be seen that the colours cannot be put in discrete sets but form a continuous gradation from the lightest to the darkest. This activity can also be used with an 'all white'; class to show that, in fact, they are not all the same colour. However, this activity would be inappropriate where there is only a small minority of black or Asian children in the class as it would only reinforce any ideas of the separateness of 'races'.

There are a few practical points arising out of this activity. Firstly, it is easier to match skin colour if the children test their paints on their arms or the backs of their hands. Secondly, the children will notice that the colours appear different when painted onto paper and when the paint dries. This could lead on to other investigations involving different coloured papers and different types of paint. The activity could be made more objective by measuring the amounts of the different paints used; however, this is very difficult. Following the comparison of colour activity, the children could go on to use the colours to paint portraits of themselves. Skin colour is only one example of continuous variation. Eye and hair colour are other examples which can be demonstrated in a similar way – except, of course, that the children cannot test out their colours directly on their eyes and hair!

There are countless examples of continuous variation in physical and other characteristics that children can explore. There are also examples of non-continuous variation which children will come across such as the ability to tongue-roll and the possession of fixed or free earlobes. In non-continuous variation an individual either has the characteristic or not – there is nothing in between. None of these is confined to a particular group of people. An interesting example of this is blood grouping (although few children will be aware of their own blood group). There are four discrete blood groups O, A, B and AB. There can be nothing in between. Everyone has one of them. All large populations will contain all of these groups although the proportion of people in each may vary. (However, this cannot lead to practical work since blood sampling is not permitted in schools!)

A question could be posed to children asking them: 'Are we alike in more ways than we are different?' – this would give them plenty of scope for investigation.

HELP CHILDREN TO BECOME ANTIRACIST AS THEY BECOME SCIENTIFIC
- Ask children to look for similarities between each other.
- Teach children about continuous variation.

Language

Language plays an important role in science. One reason for this is that many scientific words also have a meaning in everyday speech. Work, energy, force, stress . . . are words that we often use. Yet in science they have a different and very precise meaning.

Everyday usage of a word such as 'energy' may lead children to conflicting ideas about energy:

'Food gives you energy.'

'Grown-ups often don't feel energetic after meals so food takes energy away from them.'

'Taking exercise gives you energy because you feel energetic while you are doing it.'

'You use up energy when you run because you feel tired afterwards.'

It is, therefore, important to know what children are thinking before attempting a project on energy, so that they can be given suitable experiences to help them develop the scientific concept. This can be a problem to all children but especially to children for whom English is their second language. The difference between scientific language and everyday speech must be discussed with children as they arise. For example, words like force and energy are used in various everyday contexts but have specific meanings in science.

Science work cards may present a problem to children who are unable to read in English or who find reading difficult. An exercise which demonstrates to children the difficulties of deciphering a foreign language is to set them a problem with the key words written in either a language unknown to them or a made-up language.

Bobbing Podnobdobers

1. Measure out 40 cm³ of rageniv and place it in a slagup.
2. Put a humiphot of nahco into the rageniv and girot.
3. Drop 5 podnobdobers into the slagup.
4. What happens to the podnobdobers?
5. Describe your tnemirepxe to a friend and explain why the podnobdobers bobbed.

(Provide the children with: some raisins; a bottle of vinegar; a tall glass; a small teaspoon; a measuring cylinder; some bicarbonate of soda. If necessary, you can label these Rageniv, Slagup, Nahco, etc.).

It is always important for children to discuss their scientific activities with each other and with their teacher because talking helps children to refine their ideas. Where there is more than one child with English as their second language and using the same first language, they should be encouraged to talk to each other about what they are doing in their mother tongue. One of the advantages of science is that, although it is dependent on language, children can still learn scientific skills and ideas through using their mother tongue.

In the traditional secondary school the way of presenting findings of scientific activities is to write about them. Children whose first language is not English (as well as children with learning difficulties) may find this particularly difficult. Therefore, do not always expect children to present their findings in writing. There are many other ways of doing it. First of all, talking or making tape recordings may be the best way of communicating. If children in a group collaborate on this then it is less daunting. Non-verbal ways of presenting scientific work can include: drawing; painting, making models; displaying; mime; dance; taking photographs; etc. Methods that include both verbal and non-verbal elements include: annotated drawing/diagrams; setting up exhibitions; making videos; drama; etc.

Helping children with English as their second language to succeed in science will help them to gain confidence through the experience of success. More ideas for this are suggested in Chapter 4.

HELP CHILDREN TO BECOME ANTIRACIST AS THEY BECOME SCIENTIFIC
- Encourage children to talk about their scientific ideas and activities.
- Avoid work cards that will not be understood by the children you want to use them.
- Allow children to use their mother tongue when discussing their scientific ideas.
- Value non-verbal communication of scientific activities.

Raising children's awareness of racism

One objective in teaching children science is to help them to become progressively more critical. They are expected to learn to assess their own scientific activities and those of their peers. It is only in this way that they can learn to develop their skills and abilities. This critical awareness can be extended to published materials (books, posters, schemes of work cards and computer programs) and to scientific programmes on TV and video. With their teacher's help, children can develop methods of evaluating scientific materials. A simple example would be to count the number of people of different ethnic origins depicted in a book or on a programme. In a large number of books the pictures show only Europeans. A more sophisticated evaluation would look at what the people were engaged in. In many biology books black and Asian people are only depicted as suffering from malnutrition. How many books show black doctors, scientists or engineers? How many scientific TV programmes or videos are introduced by Asian or black scientists? Children could also devise other methods for detecting Eurocentricity in published materials and programmes.

Unfortunately, too many published materials fail to be multicultural although many publishers are beginning to be aware of this. So, what can children do about the problem? They cannot throw away all the racist books (though this must be done with the worst) – books are very expensive and most schools have little money to spare. Firstly, children can voice their criticisms to each other and to their teachers. Secondly, they can write to publishers to let them know what is not acceptable in scientific learning materials. Thirdly, they can do the same as Sean and Darren were doing in the introduction to this chapter – that is, cutting out suitable pictures to stick over ones they considered unsuitable.

With older children their awareness of racism can be further raised by surveying the attitudes of people in newspapers and magazines.

HELP CHILDREN TO BECOME ANTIRACIST AS THEY BECOME SCIENTIFIC

- Make children aware of overt and covert racism.
- Teach children to be critical – of themselves and other people, of published materials, computer programmes and TV and videos.
- Throw out racist learning materials.
- Ask children to substitute pictures and names in published materials that are not antiracist.
- Challenge racism yourself and teach children to do so.

Appropriate technology

Appropriate technology is sometimes regarded as 'low' technology and therefore inferior to 'high' technology. But is it? By studying some of the appropriate technology that is often used in developing countries children can learn that it requires a high degree of ingenuity and that the cost to the environment – and to the people making it – is far lower. In addition, the scientific principles on which it is based are often fairly simple and within the understanding of most primary age children, so they can tackle 'real' science problems. Examples are described in Chapter 10.

The fridge

A simple fridge can be made by placing a tin in a reservoir of water and covering it with a piece of cloth which dips into the reservoir. The cloth acts as a wick, drawing up the water. Water evaporates from the cloth taking heat from the tin and from the air inside it. A more sophisticated design includes wire netting supported by a wooden framework surrounding the side of the tin and with a reservoir on top. Charcoal is placed between the wire netting and the tin and the cloth wicks carry water from the reservoir to the charcoal. As the water evaporates from the charcoal so the air inside the tin is cooled. The advantage of using charcoal is that it provides a large area for evaporation. Having made one of these fridges children can investigate ways of improving their design. For example, are there any other materials that could replace the charcoal and be more effective? Another line of enquiry would be to look at the optimum conditions for using the fridge, or to look for situations in which fridges are essential (such as for medicines in hot climates).

The haybox

Hayboxes have been used for slow cooking for centuries all over the world. The idea is that some food is heated to boiling point in a saucepan with a lid, then put in a large container with hay between the container and the covered saucepan and more hay put on top before the lid is closed. The food will then go on cooking for several hours as heat loss is minimised by the insulating hay. Children can investigate ways of making the best haybox and can devise fair tests to see whether other materials could insulate better than hay.

HELP CHILDREN TO BECOME ANTIRACIST AS THEY BECOME SCIENTIFIC
- Use appropriate technology as a basis for scientific activities.
- Help children to value appropriate technology.
- Let them tackle 'real' technological problems at their level.

Scientific ideas

Scientific ideas can sometimes explain why there are different customs in other lands. For instance, some differences in clothing depend on climate and some differences in building materials and designs depend on climate and the probability of earthquakes. Investigations based on these ideas can help children to understand reasons for such differences.

Here is an example of a simple experiment to show the different insulating properties of various clothing materials. Collect several plastic squeezy bottles or lemonade bottles and let children cover each in a different fabric, e.g. wool, cotton, nylon, artificial fur and silk. Leave one bottle uncovered. Fill each with hot water at the same temperature. Let children take the temperature of each at five-minute intervals, or more simply after half an hour. Compare the results and ask them to explain. Two safety points to remember: if the water is very hot make sure that the teacher pours it and checks that it cannot be spilt; and always use alcohol-in-glass thermometers.

Children could then plan their own way of finding out which materials keep things cool longest.

HELP CHILDREN TO BECOME ANTIRACIST AS THEY BECOME SCIENTIFIC
- Use scientific ideas to help children understand customs in other lands.

The whole school science policy

This chapter has suggested many ways in which a teacher can help to make her science teaching antiracist, and she may well add to this list of antiracist strategies. But the good that one teacher in a school can do on her own may be limited to the class of children that she teaches, and to the example she may set to others in the school. For multicultural and antiracist strategies to be really sucessful, the whole school must work together (see Chapter 7). The best way to do that is to include all those involved with a school (teachers, ancillary staff, caretaker, cooks, governors, parents and guardians) to take part in formulating and implementing an antiracist school policy in science. (In many cases this would form part of a cross-curricular, antiractist school policy.)

Science, because of its intrinsic interest to children, because of the areas of knowledge it covers, because of its links across the curriculum, and because of the teaching and learning methods it uses, is an excellent vehicle for antiracist teaching. Therefore, one important antiracist strategy is to ensure that all children learn science and learn it from as early an age as possible. Fortunately, Science is now a core subject within the National Curriculum, beginning with 5-year-olds and 11-year-olds in 1989 and progressing up the school. But children can start learning to be scientific from the nursery – and before!

Another antiracist strategy is to present children with role models of people from different cultures. Invite people from different ethnic backgrounds who pursue scientific careers to come into classrooms to talk with children about their work. Also, make sure that all children in a class get the opportunity to present their scientific findings both to children and parents in their own and in other classes – as personal presentations and displays of work. Teachers and children may also like to ensure that any work presented reflects the backgrounds of all the children who have worked on it.

An antiracist school science policy could include all the areas that have already been discussed above, including: the nature of science; resources and starting points; ideas of 'race'; language; raising children's awareness; appropriate technology; and scientific ideas. This list is not exhaustive and teachers may well find other areas which they can consider in their school policy.

HELP CHILDREN TO BECOME ANTIRACIST AS THEY BECOME SCIENTISTS
- Work together to build a whole-school, antiracist science policy.
- Include teachers, ancillary workers, caretakers, cooks, governors, parents and guardians in formulating and implementing the school antiracist science policy.
- Encourage scientists and engineers with various ethnic origins, to visit the school and talk to the children.
- Make sure that displays are multicultural.
- Make sure that children of all ethnic backgrounds are encouraged to present their scientific findings to others in the school.
- Start science as early as possible.

Chapter 2

The Multicultural Dimension in the Science of Food

Chris Hannon

Introduction

The work described below was undertaken with a class of 9-year-olds in Medway Junior School, which is situated in the inner city area of Leicester. The environment of Medway Junior consists largely of terraced housing, and is one of the main multi-ethnic areas of the city. The school itself is a typical Victorian two-storey building with a large central hall and classrooms on all sides. It has 290 pupils of whom approximately 50% are Muslim, 30% Hindu, 10% Sikh and 10% Christian, the main languages being Gujerati, Urdu, Bengali, Punjabi and English. The school staff, most of whom are English, are assisted by a number of bilingual support teachers and other adults from the local community, and there are close links with tutors and students from the nearby School of Education at Leicester University.

In this particular term, our chosen topic for the 9-year-olds was food, and in planning my work I had been influenced by an earlier Science Workshop TV programme on 'Fruits and Vegetables'. The programme had encouraged a cross-curricular approach, blending science and art work through close observation and depiction of real fruits and vegetables, and was organised around the contents of a market barrow. However, there was no multicultural dimension to the programme: the examples on the barrow were cucumbers, bananas, apples, beans, etc., the everyday produce available in any market or greengrocers throughout Britain. I wanted to use the programme, but at the same time, I wanted to approach the topic from a multicultural perspective, in line with the school's philosophy.

So I set up a display of fruit and vegetables which I bought literally next door to the school in the local Asian and Caribbean shops and markets. All these foods are, of course, in everyday use in the children's homes; they were unusual, 'exotic', only to me. The children enjoyed knowing much more about the foods than I did.

In the display I chose produce most likely to be used in the children's homes. These were karela, okra, sugar apples, valor, guava, plantains, mangoes, gourds, tura and savasos, as well as the usual bananas, apples, cucumbers, etc. I was pleased with the display. The grocer was extremely patient with me and labelled each fruit or vegetable on the front of the brown paper bags. This enabled me to label the produce on display. But this was all I knew about the fruits! I had no idea what was inside these wonderfully shaped foods. I could have dissected the foods beforehand but I decided against this, as I wanted genuinely to learn from and with the children, reversing the roles of teacher and pupil.

As soon as the children saw the display there was great excitement. They immediately began to tell me the names of the produce in their own language. They explained how they were prepared, cooked and eaten. I found this initial discussion very interesting. The children, knowing more about the produce than myself, thoroughly enjoyed 'teaching' me. This must have been valuable in enhancing their self-esteem.

I was told that the karela is sliced and added to curries. It also cleans the blood and is good for you if you suffer from diabetes.

Gourds, larger than the one on display, are dried out and used as the sound boxes on sitars.

A Karela

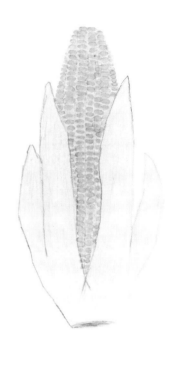

Okra, often known as ladies fingers, is also sliced and used in curries.

The savaso or 'ramfol' is known as 'Rama's fruit'. Rama was the Hindu God who married Sita. The sugar apple or custard apple is known as 'Sita's fruit'; it is cut in half to expose the soft, white flesh which can be eaten with a spoon, throwing away the large, shiny dark seeds.

The children were naming the fruits and vegetables in their mother tongue. So I asked them to label the produce in their own language. This immediately added a whole new dimension to the display.

From this beginning, several possible activities were developed, as follows:

Language activities

- naming and labelling foods in different languages
- discussions on how food is eaten
- describing the fruits, discussing shape, colour, texture, weight
- writing descriptions for others to guess the name of the fruit

Description of a fruit

The colour of this fruit is orange
The shape of this fruit is a sphere
The fruit is quite dotty
There is a piece of broken twig on the top
It's quite soft and quite ~~rough~~
It's got a air freshing smell.

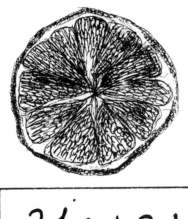

21ct21

Science activities

- predicting the nature of the inside of the fruit (texture, colour, seeds)
- classifying the foods in whatever way they chose and giving reasons for their groupings
- observing changes over a period of time
- measuring changes in weight over time
- drawing cross-sectional cuts of fruits
- growing the seeds obtained from them
- preserving fruits, e.g. preventing bananas from going brown

Such activities show how closely related science is to language when we begin to develop a multicultural dimension in teaching, particularly when displaying and recording observations. This point is further developed in Chapter 4.

Before showing the 'Science Workshop' programme to the class, I asked them, working in pairs, to look at the display and to put the produce into groups in any way they wished, selecting as many groups as they thought were necessary. I felt it was important to see how they would attempt to do this.

There were some interesting classifications. The most predictable was the 'fruits–vegetables' grouping; when I asked how they knew what was a fruit and what was a vegetable, they explained that, for example, they knew the karela didn't taste sweet or 'fruity', and as far as they were concerned, fruit tasted sweet and was eaten for dessert, whereas a vegetable was eaten with meat. Other classifications include 'above ground–below ground' and 'green–not green'.

The children now were beginning to use basic skills such as looking for patterns, similiarities and differences, so at this point I showed the programme to them, to introduce other ideas of fruit and vegetable classification. Botanists classify fruits as having seeds and growing from a flower. The children were amazed that tomatoes, karelas, okra, peas and beans are in fact fruits according to scientists. They also learned that 'vegetable' is a cook's word for classifying produce. The programme stresses, however, that both classifications are 'correct', because they are related to the culture and context in which they are used. I felt it was important to stress that the children's classifications were valuable as an activity, even though they did not have the same results as the TV programme.

Observation and Dissection

After watching the part of the programme dealing with observing and dissecting the fruit and vegetables, I asked the children to choose a fruit or vegetable from the display. They had, in pairs, to look carefully at it and make notes about its appearance, referring to its shape, size, texture and colour. They later had to describe the plant to the class without revealing its name. The children in the class had to look at the display and identify the plant from the description.

I found this language/science task an effective way of helping the children to observe more carefully because they knew they had an audience to relate to and this gave a purpose for accurately recording their observations.

I then asked the children to predict the nature of the inside of the fruit or vegetable before dissecting it. They needed to look for clues before making their prediction. I noticed one child picking up a mango and pressing it with his thumb and forefinger. I asked him why he was doing this and he explained he had seen his mum on many occasions doing this to fruit to see if it was ripe. Another was shaking her fruit to see if it had liquid inside it. 'Similar to shaking a coconut,' she explained.

I found these techniques, using various senses such as listening, touching and testing, interesting as well as the additional skills picked up by observing their parents.

We dissected, observed and drew or painted in one afternoon session. The children worked in pairs, sharing a hand lens, scalpel and cutting board. Each group kept the fruit or vegetable which they had previously observed and made predictions about it. I gave them the freedom to cut either cross-sectionally or along its length. I warned them, however, to think before they sliced! They could not repair mistakes with a tube of glue.

I stressed the safety factors: for example, when using scalpels it is important to cut down on to a board and away from fingers.

The aim of the observation is to gather as much detail as possible. It is here that the hand lens is important. The TV programme explains how to use a hand lens correctly: the lens is held close to the eye and the object is moved up to the lens until it comes into focus. The children were actively encouraged to discuss their observations and review their findings after discussion. I asked questions such as:

Can you see. . .?
Do you notice. . . .?
What shape is. . . .?
Can you recognise any patterns?
What size is. . . .?
What colour is. . . .?
How is this like this?
How is this different from this?

When we started to record our observations, we found that we had a perfect opportunity to blend both artistic and scientific skills. The children had art materials such as pastels, paints and sketching pencils to record their findings. I asked them to choose an appropriate medium which would effectively represent their observations, and this resulted in work of a very high standard, revealing just how closely they had observed.

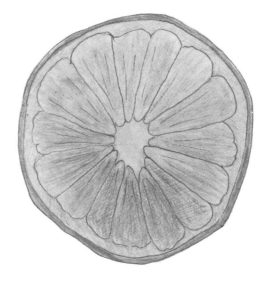

An Orange

Extending the activities

The topic was into its third week at this stage and we had gone through several changes in the fruit and vegetable display.

Some of the produce had to be changed several times because of drying out. The karela looks very sad after a few days. It loses its shine, wilts and eventually turns black. However, new produce appeared on the display: children brought in items without mentioning it. Dissecting, of course, necessitates replenishing of the stock.

It was the 'shrivelling up' of the karela which prompted the children to ask why this was happening. On thinking through the problem they suggested it might be because it is losing water. They therefore decided to measure the water lost by weighing the karela when it was bought and then re-weighing it to see if there was any change.

They talked about how they could keep the karela fresh. The children made a list of the ways they had seen their parents keep fruit and vegetables fresh:

- placing in fridge or storing in a cool place
- wrapping in silver foil
- wrapping in layers of newspaper.

Having prepared the list I asked them if they could design a 'fair test' to see if their suggestions for keeping things fresh worked.

Paramita Kuswandi

Korella

On Friday we weighed a fresh korella. We left it over the weekend and re-weighed it on Monday. We predicted on Friday what might happen to the korella.
I think the korella is going to be lose weight after two days because the korella is mouldy and its getting the juice away.

After discussion it was decided that each karela would be first weighed then placed in one of the conditions suggested for keeping them fresh. They realised they would need a 'control', i.e. a karela kept in normal conditions, to compare their results with.

Some children then decided to try to grow seeds from the dissected fruits. We turned a failed attempt at growing karela seeds into a successful field trip for some of the children in the class. The children could not germinate the karela or okra seeds, so rather than submit to failure I contacted the University's botanical gardens and arranged a visit for six children. They were going to interview a member of staff there to see if they could find out how to grow karela and okra plants. The children had to prepare their questions before the visit, take notes of the interview and report back to the rest of the class on return to school. The children saw many fruit and vegetables growing which they normally only saw on the grocer's shelf. Unfortunately, the staff had never grown karelas or okras. They suggested growing them in hot, humid conditions, which is difficult to do in the cool classrooms of our school!

Cross-Curricular Work

Our topic in maths at the time was percentages, and I was trying to use practical ideas to help the children understand the concept. I decided to involve our fruit and vegetable work.

The children counted 100 methi (fenugreek) seeds and placed them in a petri-dish of damp cotton wool. The percentage of germinated seeds would be calculated after a few days. (Fenugreek is a spice widely used in

Staying Fresh

We wanted to find out what the best conditions were for keeping our karella's fresh. We took seven karellas and weighed them when they were fresh. We then put them to store in different places over one week. Here are the results.

results

	wt when fresh.	wt after the week	description of karellas after a week.
1. control	87g	21g	fungus
2. fridge	50g	42g	green
3. silver foil	30g		liquified
4. silver foil + fridge	40g	40g	green / fresh
5. wrapping paper	45g	23g	fungus
6. cool dark place	45g	30g	yellow / dry
7. polythene bag	46g		liquid

We found that the best conditions for storing karellas were wrapped in silver foil in the fridge.

Asian cookery; it is extremely inexpensive to buy, and has similar quick germinating properties to mustard or cress.)

Further involvement with other aspects of the curriculum was ensured by discovering the origins of the fruit and vegetables. The atlas helped us to locate the sources of some of the produce. The children also interviewed the grocer to find out where he obtained the produce from. We discovered that the okra is grown in India. The karela is grown in both Cyprus and Kenya. Guava and valor are grown in Kenya. The children then identified these countries in an atlas. I found this activity useful in developing oral and interview skills. I found that it was more effective to allow only two or three children to interview the grocer rather than invade the shop with a class of children. This activity also served to impress upon them that these plants do not suddenly appear on the grocer's shelf. Each piece of fruit or vegetable has a global story to tell.

I came across other interesting activities which we might have done had there been time. For instance, Fisher and Hicks *World Studies 8–13* (1985) features a Case Study on Bananas, which looks at how and where they are grown, and how the grower does not receive a fair price for his produce. The point is made by small group activities and performing a play/simulation.

Conclusion

The work described above has carried on in various forms, and has aroused great interest amongst the class as a whole. It may be objected that I was fortunate in having a local supply of 'multicultural' fruits, but many of these are now available in most supermarkets throughout the country. Nor did it require researching a great deal of background information on my part: on the contrary, one of the motivating features for the children was that I was also learning, and that they had something to teach me. The topic also illustrated how children initiate their own scientific enquiry once they are enthused by what they are doing.

And what if my class is all white and doesn't know about such things either? As Jasbir Mann shows in Chapter 3, the same principles apply, the only difference being that teachers and children will need to go to other sources than themselves and their parents for information; to shopkeepers, cookery books or wherever. The important point is for the teacher to treat all materials as equally valid, equally interesting, equally worthy of study, in the spirit of a genuine desire to explore scientifically.

Note

A list of some Leicester stockists of ethnic minority artefacts, clothes, food, etc., is available on request from the editor, University of Exeter School of Education, St Luke's, Exeter EX1 2LU.

Chapter 3

Teaching Science Multiculturally in All-white Primary Schools

Jasbir Mann

Following the Swann Report (DES, 1985a), many publications have stressed the multicultural nature of schools and society, and the increasing interdependence of cultures and nations.The educational system has been encouraged to acknowledge this, both in the curriculum and in the organisation and operation of its institutions.

In curriculum terms, the reports of the National Curriculum Science Working Group were generally found to be positive and sensitive to these issues. For example, in the Final Report to the Secretary of State (National Curriculum Science Working Group, 1988), the section on 'Science and Cultural Diversity' accepts and promotes concerns which are both multicultural (for example, using pupils' social and linguistic cultural experiences) and antiracist (for example, providing the flexibility which allows pupils to build their confidence and self-esteem). This is a major step forward from the earlier statement of Policy (DES, 1985b), as Mike Watts discusses in Chapter 8. But we still have to ask, what is it we are actually presenting to children?

In this respect, the guidance from the DES in its book *National Curriculum: From Policy to Practice* (DES, 1989a) is not helpful, since it makes reference only to the need to 'cover' gender and multicultural issues across the curriculum without providing guidance on what this means in practice.

For example, many 'all-white' schools have in the past operated as though multicultural education was not relevant to them, seeing it as merely providing help to ethnic minority children in inner city schools. And yet multicultural education is relevant to all schools, perhaps more so where children all originate within the dominant white cultures.

Early in 1989, I was fortunate to have an opportunity to do some systematic work in a small village school in Leicestershire. During the previous two years, I had been involved in running a series of workshops for primary teachers aimed at helping them tackle science in a multicultural way, and these workshops had developed ideas for activities with children on topics such as utensils, keeping cool, musical instruments, windmills. Further information about the workshops can be found in more detail elsewhere (Mann *et al.*, 1988). However, I had not previously had a chance to try all of these out myself with children so I decided on this occasion to trial these activities in the school.

I worked with a class of 8–9-year-olds, and began by trying to find out how they saw science and scientists. I asked them to draw a picture of 'a scientist' and write down what they thought a scientist did. As Barbara Wyvill also reported in Chapter 1, most of them drew a white male scientist with names like 'Professor Doom', who 'invented' and 'experimented with computers'.

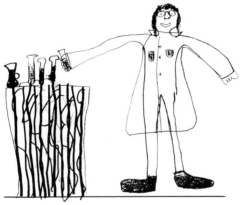

This offered me the opportunity to show pictures and examples of women as well as men from all ethnic and racial backgrounds 'doing' science. We have to ensure that examples are drawn from different cultures as often as possible, to prevent children developing stereotypical images of black people as starving victims, or of their cultures as less 'civilised'.

In the second lesson, I chose to focus on utensils. The earlier workshops had led to the creation of a utensil kit, consisting of cooking utensils of all kinds from various Asian and African origins, most of which are in regular use in homes in Leicester. Also in the kit were photographs of utensils, and sheets of ideas for activities, for both infant and junior children.

I first introduced the class to a variety of utensils: great interest was shown. As many were outside their experience, we spent a lot of time talking about them and guessing what they could be used for, taking into account their shape, size and materials from which they were made. I then asked the children to choose one of the utensils, draw it and write down their observations.

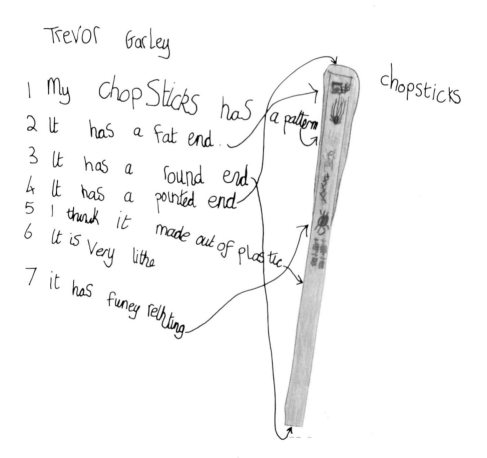

Trevor Garley

1 My Chop Sticks has a pattern
2 It has a fat end.
3 It has a round end.
4 It has a pointed end.
5 I think it made out of plastic.
6 It is very litho
7 it has funey relhting

chopsticks

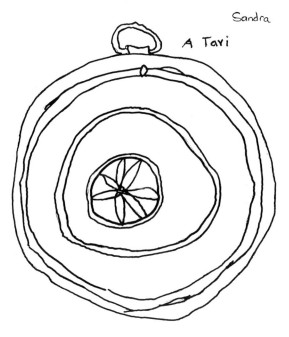

Sandra

A Tavi

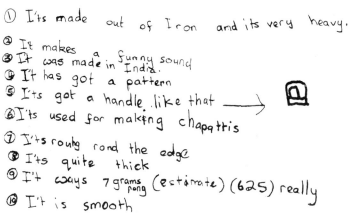

① I'ts made out of Iron and its very heavy.

② It makes a funny sound
③ It was made in India.
④ It has got a pattern
⑤ I'ts got a handle like that ——→ 🔲
⑥ I'ts used for making chapattis

⑦ I'ts rough rond the edge
⑧ I'ts quite thick
⑨ I't ways 7 grams pong (estimate) (625) really
⑩ I't is smooth

In the lessons which followed, we carried out other activities from the junior sheet in the kit, involving estimating weight, measuring how much various utensils could hold, reflections in their surfaces, etc. On one occasion, I produced a matrix for analysing each utensil, and encouraged a group of children to fill it in by observing chosen utensils, as illustrated on the next page.

Elizabeth

MATRIX / GRID — some possible uses of a grid.

UTENSILS + VESSELS	A	B	C	D	E
MATERIALS	Steel	Steel	Steel	Steel Glass	Steel
USES	eating	Storeing Food	eating	drinking	eating
E + A SIZE/ MEASUREMENTS (+Comparisions)	length 21 cm	C 39 cm	C 32 cm	C 22 cm	C 62 cm
SHAPE	Oval long	round	round	cone	round
E + A WEIGHT	55 g	155 g	55 g	150 g	550 g
E + A VOLUME/ CAPACITY	10 ml	500 ml	150 g	250 ml	500 ml
FEEL / TOUCH	Smooth	Smooth	smooth	Smooth	Smooth
COLOUR	Silver	Silver	Silver	Silver	Silver
DIFFERENT CULTURAL USES	Soup	Cooking	Chop Sticks	eating	drinking

E + A = Estimation + Actual

The matrix was useful in that it helped identify areas that we needed to spend more time on, for example estimating, weighing and measuring volume. Some children gained enjoyment and satisfaction from repeating their observations on several utensils, whilst others were satisfied to explore just one. Here, the sets of photographs were useful for classification and sorting activities.

By this stage, we had spent quite a lot of time handling the utensils and the children were curious about how they were actually used. So in one lesson, we decided to use the rolling pin, board and tava to make chapattis. The children enjoyed doing this, and wrote up the process in their own way.

As a result of working with the children in this way the headteacher suggested that other schools in the locality might be interested. Since there were regular meetings within the cluster to share ideas, he proposed that it would be appropriate for the next meeting of the group to focus on developing a multicultural dimension in science.

A session was set up which was attended by ten teachers. I chose to structure this by dealing with the three issues which we had addressed in our workshops over the previous two years, namely:

1   When we organise science lessons, how can we make sure that we

acknowledge and promote the cultural diversity of the classroom, school, community and society?

2   What specific language demands does science make on our children?

3   What resources are available to help us get started?

To these concerns, the teachers added a further, relating to

4   How does this approach fit in with the attainment targets for science?

The teachers stressed from the beginning that in developing their multicultural policies, their schools had encountered difficulties with science and maths. So as an introductory activity, a set of discussion cards was used, each of which contained a statement and illustration to stimulate discussion and encourage teachers to articulate their views concerning science and its place in a multicultural curriculum. The six statements on the cards were:

- 'Science is neutral and culture free.'
- 'Language issues are irrelevant in the study of science.'
- 'The contribution of the East to world scientific development has been minimal.'
- 'It is impossible to combine scientific process and skills within a multicultural approach.'
- 'We need a view of science which ignores differences and emphasises similarities.'
- 'Issues of race and inequality would be inappropriate in a science curriculum.'

The points made by the teachers arising out of their discussions were as follows:

- Scientists are human beings who come from a certain cultural and ethical background, and therefore cannot be totally culture free.
- Innovations are made by people, and scientific research can be directed by people who fund research.
- Science reflects the values of the community among whom it originates (see Chapters 9 and 10)

'Science is neutral and culture free.'

- We should not isolate science or scientific views from lay people and children by using an isolated register.
- Science has to be related to the everyday understandable world of pupils and to build on their previous experiences, knowledge, language concepts and ideas.
- Before pupils meet scientific jargon, they need to use their own language to handle concepts (see Chapter 4).

'Language issues are irrelevant in the study of science.'

- Non-European science is almost ignored. We never see examples of black scientists.
- Why is it that we have only now heard of McCoy, Woods, Drew, Raman? Why are Indian achievements not in the textbooks? (see Chapter 5)

'The contribution of the East to world scientific development has been minimal.'

'It is impossible to combine scientific process and skills within a multicultural. approach.'

- We have never tried this. How do we do it?
- The National Curriculum suggests some areas where we might begin (diet, energy, health, ecosystems etc.).
- What are the multicultural issues we need to bear in mind? (see Chapter 5)

- Science always tends to focus on differences: only by understanding them can prejudices based on ignorance be dismantled. To ignore difference is in essence unscientific.
- Primary age children need to build a positive self-image and only then can they respect others. So similarities and differences need to be tackled (see Chapter 1).

'We need a view of science which ignores differences and emphasises similarities.'

'Issues of race and inequality would be inappropriate in a science curriculum.'

- 'Scientific' arguments have in the past been used to justify theories of inequality. It is up to scientists and teachers of science to reject the notion of superiority and inferiority of human beings based on physical features and skin colour (see Chapter 1).

As a result of these discussions, the group had in their first meeting little time to look at the materials in detail, so follow-up sessions were suggested which would provide an opportunity for the teachers to try out ideas with small groups of children. It was finally agreed that two further afternoon sessions would be held, and that for these each teacher would bring a group of 4–5 children from their own class, to try the activities.

WORKSHOP LAYOUT

KEEPING COOL
Panjati fans
Chinese fans
Umbrellas
Turban
Clay pot

MUSICAL INSTRUMENTS
Sitar
Sarangi
Tabla
Dholak
Sansa (thumb piano)
Talking drum
Finger cymbols
Chimta
Chmenneh
Ghungarooes
Ektara
Harmonium
Bansuri

FOOD
Food photographs
Books
Jars containing spices etc.

WORK AREA

BLACK SCIENTISTS
Booklet – *Scientist* (Science
Curriculum Review, 1985)
Poster set from CIBA-GEIGY
'Black Scientist'

OURSELVES – 'RACE'
Photographs – Black and white
of adults & children
Series of books called
    Look at Hands   by Ruth
    Look at Eyes   Thomson
    Look at Faces   Henry
    Look at Feet   Pluckrose
    Look at Teeth
(Published by Franklin Watts)
Paints

UTENSILS
Thali – stainless steel, plastic
Steel pans – different sizes
Tava – large,medium, small
Steel glasses – different sizes
Tiffin
Ladles
Steel bowl

FESTIVALS
Longman **Science** Scheme
Festival packs
e.g. Diwali
    Valsakhi
    Chinese New Year, etc.
Candles
Incense

All the activities were arranged as a 'circus' in the (small!) school hall. The diagram on p. 47 shows the activities which were set out. Each activity had with it a set of materials and a brief workcard with a suggested 'starter', linked to one attainment target.

In each of the two sessions, there were five teachers each with 4–5 children covering both infant and junior age ranges. Each group spent 40 minutes on an activity, then moved on with its teacher to another, although one group of 6–7-year-olds spent most of the afternoon with the 'Food' box!

The value of these sessions was that it enabled teachers to try out some of the topics with a small group, before trying them with an entire class.

The workcard for the 'Race' activities

```
OURSELVES - RACE
----------------

Attainment target 2: the variety of life
----------------------------------------

Attainment target 4: genetics and evolution
-------------------------------------------

How sensitive are your fingertips?

Touch a friend with the points of two
cocktail sticks.

Can she/he feel one or two?

Try again with the points closer together.

Get your friend to test you.

How can you make this a fair test?


Mix your own skin colour

Which paints did you use?

How could you make this quantitative?

You will need:- black, white, red, blue and
                yellow paint; a pot of water;
                brushes; palettes; paper.
```

The teachers involved had already been part of a 'cascade' programme to raise awareness about the need to widen their curriculum and tackle discrimination. They found these follow-up sessions valuable because the activities were clearly linked to attainment targets, and because the opportunity to work with their own children allowed them to get more out of the activities. Most teachers went away convinced that they could fit this work into their normal topic-based approach, and some have booked out the kits of materials to try them out with their own classes this term.

Interestingly, whilst the children were initially more interested in the large, spectacular materials such as the sitar, the potential of these was

The workcard for the 'Food' activities

```
FOOD
----

Attainment target 3: Processes of life
--------------------------------------

How many of these food samples do you recognise?

Do you know any alternative names for them?

Where do they come from?

What are they like inside? (Predict and cut).


Identify the smells?

"Smelling" jars containing spices and herbs



What are the ingredients used to make a Mars bar?

Where do they come from?

Why is this?


In what ways are these breads a) similar
                             b) different?

You will need:- pitta bread, wholemeal bread,
                chapattis, cholla, hand lens,
                microscope, knife, board, plates.
```

not as great as the smaller, simpler activities such as the spice boxes and skin cards.

A common discussion point was the lack of information about where to obtain things, and therefore lists of stockists were produced (see footnote on p. 37). Other background resources were listed such as the Ciba-Geigy series of posters on 'Black Scientists'.

The work has shown that teachers and children in all-white, rural schools are interested and motivated by science activities which have this added dimension. Moreover, teachers with knowledge and interest in other cultures can play a vital role in helping others to overcome that initial barrier which, whilst relatively easy to overcome, is often not tackled out of a lack of confidence.

Chapter 4

Supporting Language Learning through Doing Science

Clare Townend,
Aldona Petrenas,
Larry Street

Perceptions of 'the language of science'

My immediate response to the term 'the language of science' is one which conjures up the notion of scientific jargon: subject specific vocabulary with which I am not familiar so that I struggle with meaning, the usage and possibly the spelling. My response is that of a monolingual person operating in a situation where my mother tongue is the language of instruction. I suspect that the response of many pupils in schools would be far more complex, conjuring up not only scientific jargon, but memories of sitting through long diatribes intended to explain a certain reaction, concept, process or result, but which in fact had no meaning although the pupils had come to their own hypotheses and conclusions. Memories also of being asked to carry out tasks unsupported and consequently being unable to complete the tasks, or of getting further and further behind. Feelings such as 'if only I could do the work in my mother tongue', 'if only this worksheet was more comprehensible and clear, and I could follow the instructions', 'if only I could talk this over with someone else', or maybe less analytical responses such as 'I don't understand this, I'm going to drop the subject as soon as I can; in the meantime I'll just pretend I understand'. These more complex responses could be those of many pupils in this country in both the primary and secondary sectors, who have a first language other than English, or speak a dialect of English which is quite different from the more standard form used in schools. How do these pupils cope? How do teachers respond to the linguistic diversity which exists? And how do teachers support pupils to make the curriculum more accessible to all of them, and play a role in the linguistic development of all children?

It would seem that the science curriculum can offer great opportunities for the linguistic development as well as the conceptual development of all pupils, provided that the demands are recognised and pupils are supported in meeting them. I hope to illustrate this in the following pages, but I feel there is another area of the language of science which must be considered and which must form the foundation for this linguistic and conceptual development.

This other area emanates from my second response to the phrase 'the language of science' and is concerned with attitudes expressed through language. As a pupil, my own image of science was one which was dominated by males, indeed white males – a perception that most science or occupations related to science were the domain of men and that inventions and developments were white western achievements. I was, of course, unaware then that my perception was very narrow and in fact unrealistic, and that gender and race were issues I needed to consider, since I was educated in the tradition and institutionalism of a male-dominated ethnocentric society. My present situation causes me concern, since being aware of the issues is one thing but having power to change the situation is another, and I wonder how many other pupils are growing up in society feeling either superior or inferior, either counted or uncounted depending on their cultural heritage and gender. Many of these messages which are prejudiced and lead to discrimination are not only relayed through the choice of the content of the curriculum but also through the language which is used: the language which expresses 'them and us' situations, which refers to groups of people with different lifestyles from the perceived 'norm' in pejorative terms. Language, whether verbal or non-verbal, has a crucial role to play as a communicator of either positive or negative attitudes about different people, situations and developments. It is therefore of paramount importance that we look at our attitudes and at the language we use as a foundation for our teaching and it is within this framework of antiracism and antisexism that we look at the curriculum, what it has to offer and the demands it places on pupils.

'Subject matter teaching, when made comprehensible, is language teaching'

Whether we are subject specialists or class teachers, we should all be concerned with language development and regard this as something which takes place alongside conceptual development; indeed the two can be mutually supportive. The term 'language development' encompasses many aspects of communication; it involves skills of listening, speaking, reading, writing. Whilst all these aspects are very important, it is the area of oracy which research has shown to have often been overlooked or not given sufficient consideration. And yet oracy is crucial for the development of concepts. The teaching of science has experienced changes over the years, and clearly more recent developments have involved a shift from content and retention of facts to looking at processes and developing the skills inherent in these: skills such as researching information, observing, testing out ideas and making hypotheses. This allows pupils the opportunity to undergo an experiential learning process which is activity based. Obviously a major part of this approach involves talk, so that pupils can exchange ideas, have these ideas reinforced or challenged and collaborate in the learning process. Obviously too, for this exchange of communication to take place pupils must be in situations where they can collaborate and where the task is designed to encourage communication and cooperation. Those setting the task must also be aware of the type of language use involved in it.

Some time ago the language support service for which I work compiled a list of some of the main functions of pupils' spoken language. Its aim was to provide an overview of oral language which was manageable and could be used as a guide in the on-going appraisal of pupils' oracy skills, as well as a framework for considering what types of language use a particular activity could be expected to involve. It is interesting to set this list of functions of language alongside the National Curriculum Attainment Target 1 on Skills Development in Primary Science, since it illustrates the opportunities which the science curriculum can provide for pupils to use language for a whole variety of purposes (see table on next page).

Placing this into the context of an actual science activity it can be seen that a simple activity simultaneously provides opportunities for the development of various process skills and the use of language for different purposes, as in the following section.

Infant children's talk during science activities

The examples of talk which follow were collected whilst I was a PGCE student teacher working in two neighbouring multilingual Leicestershire schools. I was particularly interested in looking at talk in science and noted down some of the dialogues which took place so that I could make an analysis of the language being used.

Throughout I was testing out techniques aimed at enabling *all* pupils in the chosen mixed ability groups to learn science and to develop their

Science Skills and Functions of Spoken Language

Science process (AT 1)	Functions of pupils' spoken language	Examples
Questioning	Survival/self maintenance. . .	expressing needs, understanding instructions
Observing Measuring/ quantifying	Identification. . .	naming, labelling, comparing, classifying describing, predicting,
	Location in time. . .	anticipating, estimating time,
Describing		locating objects,
	Location in space. . .	prepositions, estimating distance/ direction
Interpreting	Questioning/ responding. . .	identifying question words and responding words
Recording/ reporting	Narration/ Reporting. . .	sequencing, ordering discussing a process
Searching for patterns	Reasoning. . .	recognising relationships, solving problems, analysing evidence,
Designing/ decision making	Imagination. . .	projecting into unknown situations
Manipulating		creating from previous experience

language skills, especially talking. Practical experimentation was chosen so as to fulfil the objective of 'talking oneself into understanding'.

In particular, the activities shared the following objectives:

1 Engaging children to talk about their observations and discoveries, and developing their vocabulary.
2 Promoting a multicultural view of science – investigating the variety of foods from around the world available in Britain today.
3 Valuing and encouraging use of mother tongues/dialects.

The topic area 'Food' was chosen, in particular fruit and vegetables. Resources were acquired locally and I also used the *Longman Science World* pictures. As these materials were all text-free they encouraged children to speak, and to use a variety of mother tongues. Group work was encouraged as it provided bilingual pupils with opportunities to listen to a variety of registers, especially peer registers which are more likely to be acquired by them than adult registers, and to use their mother tongues.

The experiments were analysed to see what scientific processes and language functions the activities developed, as categorised above. The scientific processes included were: observation, measuring, describing, investigating, predicting, experimenting and explaining. This approach was devised from ideas in the *Aide Memoire for Multicultural Education* (Leicestershire LEA, 1987).

The first four experiments were carried out by different groups of five/ six children from a top infant class. They shared the following objectives:

1 To develop children's abilities to observe and investigate shape, colour and texture.
2 To develop ideas about sorting and making sets, and to carry out simple ordering tasks.

A selection of various fruits and vegetables was used, including apples, tomatoes, karelas, yams, mangoes, mushrooms, oranges, potatoes, okra, onions, lychees, drumsticks and grapes.

The first two of these experiments shared the same method of looking at the selection of vegetables and fruit and asking pupils how many they recognised, whether they could name them and whether they knew the country of origin. Questions were asked about shape, size, colour, texture and smell, to help them observe accurately and interpret their observations more constructively. Foods were sorted into sets according to criteria such as shape, colour and weight. Questions of comparison and contrast were asked to identify similarities and differences. Are they all the same? How is this one like this one? How is this different from this? Questions were asked concerning number and measurement – how many/much/tall/wide/long? Are the tall ones heavier? Are the small ones lighter? Prediction was encouraged to build on future evidence – what do you think they are like inside? Recording took place by drawing a picture of the inside of a fruit or vegetable after it had been cut up.

A range of vocabulary was used when describing the fruit 'long', 'short', 'fat', 'thin', 'pointed', 'prickly', 'rough', 'smooth', and the children acquired words and expressions from each other. In identifying and labelling the fruits, use of the pupils' mother tongues was also encouraged.

The third and fourth experiments were concerned with counting seeds, the 'dropping fruit' experiment, smelling fruit, and classifying fruit and vegetables according to the pupils' own criteria.

I found that these experiments engendered much discussion, both between the pupils themselves and between the teacher and pupils. The children were all engaged at some time in the process skills I had hoped they would experience, and they were given the opportunity to actively hypothesise and think things through based on each other's experience. For example, when they identified the chilli some children could reflect on past experience and share this in the learning process:

> 'I eat them, they're lovely . . . that's green chilli, you can get bigger than that, bigger than that.'

Other responses were more anecdotal narratives:

> 'When I was 6 or 5 I used to just, my mum used to a whole mmm, tomato and I used to bite it and eat it and I used to leave the seeds. I used to make a big collection of it and I used to read books about seeds and vegetables.'

The activities allowed pupils to use language for several different purposes and share this with each other. For example, when cutting up the tomato the following dialogue took place:

> 'You can hold the scissors and bring it out with the scissors.'
> 'Push it out.'
> 'Squeeze it out.'
> 'Ugh it looks like slime.'
> 'Green, all green, green, greeny orange water.'

When observing their fruit, children worked towards accurate descriptions of what they saw:

> 'What do seeds look like?'
> 'Mmm, at the end of the seed it's got a point, a kind of point, it's round and it's got a little point.'
> 'What do cucumbers look like?'
> 'Cucumbers, they're kind of bumpy and long and they've got a point. On one side it's got a kind of point but it's not that pointed. And the other side is flat.'

and gave reasons for what happened:

> '. . . I already told you what it's like, it's round and . . . and when you try to squeeze it, it comes out it slips out of your hand because all the water, the juice inside the tomato makes it wet and slippery.'

The discussion which took place with both infants and juniors (they were involved in classifying, tasting and smelling experiments) were characterised by pupils interrupting each other, sentences rarely being finished and pupils challenging and contradicting each other's views. This exploratory talk allowed pupils to understand better the scientific concepts and acquire an experimental approach to problems. The encouragement of the use of mother tongue meant some pupils who might have felt alienated from the discussion could participate and also supported other children's discussion of concepts in English at a later time.

Taping the activities also made me aware of my own questioning techniques, and my over-zealousness to fill silences rather than giving pupils time to formulate responses and initiate questions themselves.

Language support in science lessons

The above work provided a clear insight into an example of practice which focused on the development of linguistic and conceptual skills side by side. However, for this kind of scientific enquiry based on shared learning and experience to take place, much thought had gone into classroom organisation, pedagogy, organisation of tasks and the needs of the pupils, and this was set within a context which respected and promoted the pupils' biculturalism and bilingualism.

The last decade has seen a gradual process in education of moving from 'chalk and talk' to active learning, and through a focus on language across the curriculum we see much more evidence of pupils involved in collaborative work. For pupils who are learning through the medium of a second language we have also seen a move from withdrawal to classroom support, so that developing pupils are no longer segregated from their peers nor denied access to the mainstream curriculum. The focus on collaborative and communicative learning has offered opportunities for bilingual pupils to have their language development supported through working in mixed ability groups where discussion work can take place in both English and the children's respective mother tongues, thus supporting their bilingualism (or multilingualism) and their conceptual development. Where activities are organised which allow pupils 'hands on' experiences and visual support, these provide a context for language to be meaningful. They also allow pupils at any stage of development in the English language to be involved in a non-threatening way. Pupils can be encouraged to join in verbally, but also have the right to remain silent until they feel confident to join in. This does not mean that pupils are not learning or involved, since they can gain conceptually from such experiences, make their own hypotheses, and (where other pupils share a language in common) discuss these. The move to language support in the classroom has also meant that additional staff can be made available to work alongside classroom teachers to assist those pupils who are in need of support at whatever linguistic level, and where human resources exist, to use a bilingual approach with pupils.

It is in relation to the actual tasks pupils are asked to perform that we must look at the linguistic demands made by the science curriculum. For example, many people would perhaps see specialist vocabulary as the most obvious area in science which needs attention and consideration for all pupils but particularly for bilingual pupils. We need to ask ourselves certain questions, such as how do we introduce new vocabulary? How aware are we of what language is specific to science? How much is necessary? How much is our use of specific terminology alienating pupils and not giving them access to the curriculum, be they dialect speakers of English or bilingual?

As Pauline Hoyle suggests, an antiracist approach to science teaching should help students '. . . demystify science or remove the barrier of power created by inaccessible scientific language. To do this they would wish to relate science to the everyday, understandable world of the students and to build on previous experiences, knowledge, language, concepts and ideas. Before students are confronted with scientific jargon they need to use their own language to discuss their own concepts. Once this is done, they are more likely to be able to cope with scientific concepts and can then have access to the scientific register. Also, some students may find it difficult to generalise concepts from one situation to another. If the register used to introduce a new scientific concept is totally unfamiliar to them, then they are even more unlikely to "learn" the science or to relate the scientific concepts to other situations'.

If we now consider the terminology used in instructions, explanations and information (spoken/written), we can see if the task is made more difficult through the use of ambiguous words and phrases, words used in a new context, or use of complex structures where simpler ones could be used.

Barbara Wyvill (Chapter 1) gave the following examples of words used in different context:

'. . . many scientific words also have a meaning in everyday speech. Work, energy, force, stress . . . are words that we often use. Yet in science they have a different and very precise meaning. Everyday usage

of a word such as 'energy' may lead children to conflicting ideas about
energy:
"Food gives you energy."
"Grown-ups often don't feel energetic after meals so food takes energy
away from them."
"Taking exercise gives you energy because you feel energetic while you
are doing it."
"You use up energy when you run because you feel tired afterwards."

It is, therefore, important to know what children are thinking before
attempting a project on energy so that they can be given suitable experiences to help them develop the scientific concept. This can be a problem to all children but especially to children for whom English is their
second language. The differences between scientific language and everyday speech must be discussed with children as they arise.'

When using questioning techniques, we need to structure questions in
such a way that they elicit the thought processes and responses which we
wish to develop. Do questions allow children to work together to produce
an answer and to offer as many children as possible the chance to put forward an idea which may be acceptable or adapted or developed in the
light of what others have said? Are questions open ended or closed, e.g.
How do you think the worm moves along the ground? Has the worm got
muscles in its body which allow it to move? Did your worm move?
    Finally, when making an account of a scientific activity, we must con-
sider the alternatives to a written prose account. How can we support
pupils in producing accounts of what they have observed and their conclusions or hypotheses?

Science schemes and language games

Before giving examples of language games, it might be necessary to discuss briefly some of the ideas behind them. In this way, teachers might
then appreciate the 'how' and 'why' of the games and, from examples
given, work out materials appropriate for themselves and their particular
children.
    Briefly, we need to ask:

1   What special language will the children have to learn?
2   How can the children best be helped to learn this language?

'Scientific' context and communication

At least in the primary and early secondary stages, 'scientific' language is something of a mythical beast. Whilst there may well be the beginning of a specialised vocabulary – 'thermometer', 'antenna', 'embryo', etc. – the language of the science lesson seems to be overwhelmingly commonplace or everyday.

> 'What's it like?'
> 'That one's different 'cos it's got six legs.'
> 'It's bubbling lots, Miss.'
> 'My caterpillar likes lettuce best.'
> 'How?'
> 'Why?'
> 'Let's try it this way.'

There seems no 'special' language here: indeed, *is* there a special, mysterious, exclusive 'scientific' way of looking at the world reserved only for science lessons? In everyday life, as well as in classroom subjects, children are constantly asking questions, observing similarities and differences, making guesses (forming a hypothesis), trying things out (conducting an experiment), reaching a conclusion and so on. In learning how to get on with classmates (and teachers), children observe carefully, consider (and sometimes discuss) before trying out bits of behaviour to see if they work.

Learning to read involves children in spotting similarities and differences:

in experimenting:

and in analysing:

The process is one of increasingly accurate observation, analysis and experiment until the mystery of script is solved, and so it is in all kinds of real learning. What is special about science is the increasing rigour and objectivity in which these ways of thinking are applied.

It is re-assuring to think that there are no 'strange' ways of thinking nor any 'strange' language in our science teaching. However, we still need to consider how to help children (some of whom may have difficulty with their English) to learn this 'ordinary' language plus the 'new' words that the science lesson brings along. If we consider the context of acquiring language, children first learn what words mean because of 'who's there' and/or 'what's happening'. The circumstances, or context, provide the vital clues to meaning.

The words 'mummy' . . . 'dinner' . . . and (oh dear) 'naughty' have clear meanings in particular circumstances. When children start using 'one-word sentences', it is the 'where' and 'what is happening' that makes sense of the language.

'Mummy' . . . (in front of a door that's stuck) . . . means . . . 'Mummy, open this door.'

'Mummy'. . . (when Susan is cuddling up) . . . means . . . 'Mummy, I LOVE you'.

'Mummy' . . . (when Mummy's car drives up) . . . means . . . 'Good, Mummy's here.'

or 'Oh, Mummy will see my dinner all over the floor.'

In the same way, science lessons provide a good context and many clues as to what the language is about. The children are doing experiments, or describing something, drawing diagrams, filling in tables and notes, and, above all, *talking* about what they are doing. Almost always, the language is about what is happening 'here and now'. Science lessons, themselves, are good for language learning. So language games should use the context of the lesson and build on it.

Language is not an abstract grammatical exercise; it is primarily a way of communicating, and science lessons are ideal for this sending and receiving of messages. If the children work in groups and the teacher plans the work well, children will be sharpening their skills in asking questions, discussing problems, suggesting solutions, and so on. Children can be really good teachers. Sometimes they might even give grammar lessons to their friends – in the nicest possible way! For example, Kam was talking in a group that was doing a local survey.

Kam: Every day, nine o'clock, my mother goes to his work.
Yuksal: *Her* work, Kam.
Kam: Oh yes, *her* work.

A teacher *might* have been tempted (or even thought it her/his 'duty') to explain to Kam that Cantonese has no masculine, feminine or neuter forms for pronouns, but that English has. Or even that the third person singular possessive pronoun has three forms. . .!!! Yuksal knew better how to teach his friend.

Language games should also get children actually working and talking together. If language is about messages (communication) and if situation and activity (context) give access to meaning, it seems reasonable to suppose that a good way to learn language is when:

1   Children are working and talking together on a common task
2   There are as many clues as possible to the meaning of the language

This account is, of course, in no way comprehensive but it does point out two important aspects of the process of learning a language.

The two ideas of context and communication underly all the suggestions for games which follow. The first of these is a set of games based on 'mini-beasts'. In relation to language skills, the appropriate statements of attainment within AT1 (Speaking and listening) might be:

- participate as a speaker freely and listen in a group engaged in a prescribed task (level 2)
- give and receive simple instructions and follow them, when pursuing a task as an individual or as a member of a group (level 3)

In addition to this general language use, the games and activities should provide plenty of practice in language skills closely related to science skills. There will be plenty of talk concerned with describing, comparing, contrasting, making hypotheses, experimenting and so on:

'that's got four feelers'
'It hasn't got legs . . . has it?'
'This one is bigger (slower, longer, etc.)'
'Put it over here/under this/on my . . .'
'what would it be like if . . .'

All this language will be used as things are happening, as children are doing things. Language and science activity will be enmeshed with meaning.

Make a Crystal Palace for Mini-beasts.

Use a plastic cake -box from a supermarket.

Make a few holes in the top with a big needle or a nail.

Or make one yourself from plasticine and cling film.

Make a hole in the top with scissors or a sharp knife.

Make a floor for the palace from paper or thin cardboard.
Divide the floor into 6"dining rooms."

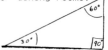

Put a dot in the middle of the floor.
Use a 60° set square to make 6 "dining rooms."

Put different things in each dining room. Put some food you like yourself like...mango...sweet potato...bits of a spring roll..
cake...chapatti...etc...BUT FIRST think what the guests might like.

* Put the palace in a cool, shaded place.

Put your "guests" in the centre of the floor.

<u>THE FIRST GUESTS</u>.
Get 10 wood lice.   If you want to be very good scientists,put a
tiny dot of paint on the back of each wood louse. Use different
colours,of course.

Every hour,or half hour, look to see where the wood lice are feeding.

<u>RECORD WHAT YOU SEE</u>.

	Where the guests are feeding.						
FOOD	9am	9.30am	10am	10.30am	11am	11.30am	12am
bread	2						
meat	4						
chapatti	3						
mango							
lettuce							
cake	1						

and so on.

You could record which coloured wood louse is feeding where by
putting coloured dots instead of numbers.

You could make a <u>Block Graph</u> to show the favourite foods.

You could make a <u>Block Graph of Favourite Foods in your Class</u>.

You could make a painting of your <u>Favourite Meal with labels on it</u>.
    Why don't you draw yourself eating it?
If you know another language,put the labels in that as well as English!!

OTHER GUESTS.

You could collect snails.

Try to get different snails.
You can call the snails after the people who brought them.

  and so on.

You could collect caterpillars.

Try to get different caterpillars.
Call the caterpillars after the children who brought them.

and so on.

NB. It's a good thing to bring some of the food the snail or caterpilla
was feeding on, then you can be sure they won't get too HUNGRY!!!!

RECORD THE RESULTS just as you did for the Wood Lice.

NOW SOME GAMES TO PLAY.

DRAW A WOOD LOUSE.   You need a dice, a pencil and paper.

To draw: the body you must throw 1.
          an antenna you must throw 2.
          all the legs you must throw 6.

DRAW A SNAIL.   To draw: the body(with the head) throw 1.
                          the shell you must throw 2.
                          an eye you must throw 3.

                          the mouth you must throw 4.
                          the tail you must throw 5.
                          a feeler you must throw 6.

YOU CAN MAKE THE SAME GAME WITH CATERPILLARS....or any other animal
          you have as a guest at the Crystal Palace.

WORD SEARCH.

How many wood lice, caterpillars and snails can you find?

w	o	o	d	l	l	o	u	s	e	c	a	t	e	r	p	i	l	l	a	r
o	t	e	p	m	t	n	s	n	a		s	n	a	i	l	m	e	m	n	
o	s	n	a	i	l	l	c	a	t	e	r	p	i	l	l	a	r	t	a	
d	l	l	o	u	s	e	e	t	i	o	s	n	a	i	l	r	b	e	r	i

s	t	a	i	m	s	n	a	i	l	l
n	s	a	i	n	l	t	a	i	l	
t	e	t	m	z	w	x	y	z	l	
s	q	i	a	m	x	m	m	m	m	
y	y	n	z	i	y	p	p	p	p	
z	s	b	t	z	l	w	t	y	z	
z	t	r	b	z	s	n	a	i	l	

Find 3 snails
One is curled up

HINDI, CHINESE, GREEK etc WORD SEARCH.

Get the children to make a word search in their own language!
They may need to take an empty word grid home and get their parents
to help.

THE 60 METRE DASH.

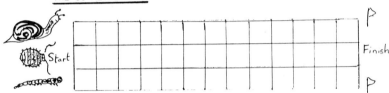

Start *Finish*

make your "animals" from card.
The children take turns to throw a dice BUT every time ANYONE throws
a 1 the snail moves one space, every time ANYONE throws a 3 the wood
louse moves one space, every time ANYONE throws a 6 the caterpillar
moves one space.

A TRACK GAME.

The children can make their *own* game with their *own* hazards and helps.

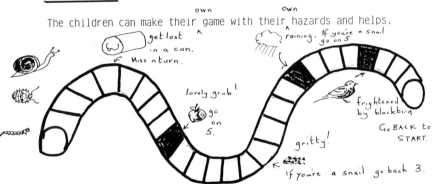

get lost in a can. Miss a turn.
raining. If you're a snail go on 5
lovely grub! go on 5.
frightened by blackbird Go BACK to START.
gritty!
If you're a snail go back 3.

The game can be with dice, but a <u>spinner</u> with things on it to do with
caterpillars, snails and wood lice will make a very interesting game.

MAKE A SPIN WHEEL.

Use a 10 cm square.   Have words like this on each section.

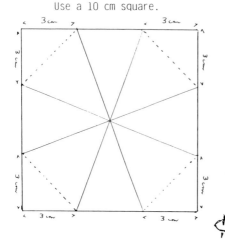
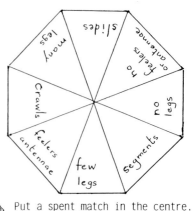

Put a spent match in the centre.

The children spin the wheel in turn. If the word/s fit the animal you have,
then you can move it one space. "few legs"...the caterpillar can move..etc.

MAKE SOME CARDS FOR YOUR TRACK GAME.

go on
6

go
back
3

lettuce

potato

okra

moves
quickly

moves
slowly

Sn---

W----
I-----

You can have
all kinds of
things on the
CARDS.

The cards are put in a pile face down. The players turn over a card in turn

ANYONE who has   an animal fitting the description on the
card can move one space.

Let's say someone turns over a card with "lettuce"...that's a favourite
food for snails...so the player with a "snail" moves one space forward.
"moves slowly" ..means ANYONE with a "snail" or a "caterpillar" can move
one space.

HOWEVER,WITH NUMBERS ONLY THE CHILD TURNING THE CARD CAN MOVE.

THE TRACK GAMES CAN HAVE INTERESTING SHAPES.

THE SNAIL TRACK GAME.

.THE CATERPILLAR TRACK GAME.

THE WOOD LOUSE TRACK GAME.

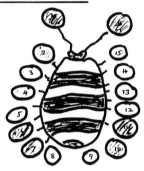

HAVE FUN!!!!!!

The above games can be seen to link with Science Attainment Target 2 (The variety of life), and in particular to the following statements of attainment:

- know that plants and animals need certain conditions to sustain life (level 2)
- understand how living things are looked after and be able to treat them with care and consideration (level 2)
- know that living things respond to seasonal and daily changes (level 3)
- be able to recognise similarities and differences among living things (level 3)

Teachers can make up games like these themselves and give them to groups of children. Workcards should be simple and as visually explicit as possible: they will in themselves be the basis for invaluable language practice as well as scientific activity. Science word searches and cross-words can be constructed , in mother tongues as well as in English. Card games or track games like the mini-beast example are also easy to con-struct, so easy that children as well as teachers can make their own. A fantastic amount of language is generated in the making and trying out of such games, even if they never play them.

The second set of games and activities is from a project on Flight. They are simple workcards concerned with making and testing aerofoils. The Egyptian glider, the Australian boomerang, the Chinese kite, all sophisti-cated forms of aerofoil, embody a clear multicultural dimension.

Experiment 1.　Making an aero foil.

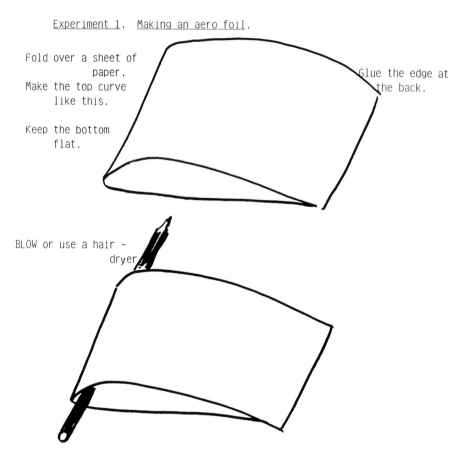

Fold over a sheet of
　　　　paper.
Make the top curve
　　like this.

Keep the bottom
　　flat.

Glue the edge at
the back.

BLOW or use a hair -
　　　dryer.

Put a pencil or a piece of wood or wire at the front.

What did you expect to happen?
What did really happen?

When you have read through the activities, it would be interesting to work out which Science and Language attainment targets these activities might contribute to, and at what levels.

Experiment 2   Is it alive?

Cut a piece of paper 4cm by 30cm.

Glue the paper to a piece of wood.

Let the glue dry.

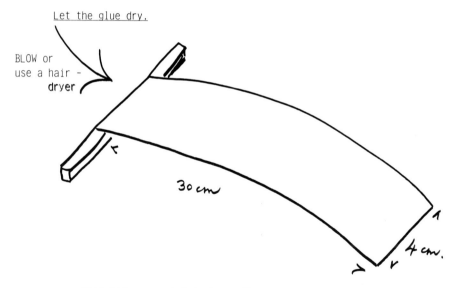

BLOW or
use a hair –
dryer

30 cm

4 cm.

What did you expect to happen?

What really did happen?

Experiment 3.   Friends or Enemies?

BLOW or use a hair dryer.

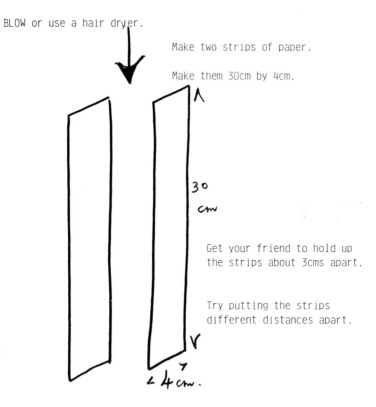

Make two strips of paper.

Make them 30cm by 4cm.

30 cm

Get your friend to hold up
the strips about 3cms apart.

Try putting the strips
different distances apart.

⌐ 4 cm.

What did you expect to happen?

What really did happen?

Did the different distances make any difference?

Experiment 4.   Table Tennis Balls.

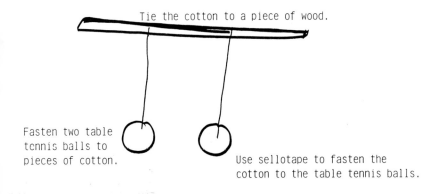

Tie the cotton to a piece of wood.

Fasten two table
tennis balls to
pieces of cotton.

Use sellotape to fasten the
cotton to the table tennis balls.

Fasten the table tennis balls about 4cms apart.

Get your friend to hold the piece of wood horizontal.

Wait until the table tennis balls are hanging still...not blowing about.

Blow between the table tennis balls using a straw......a hair dryer...
or just blowing.

What did you expect to happen?

What really did happen?

Did it make any difference when you just blew ..used a straw..
                                        used a hair dryer???

Experiment 5. A Balsa wood aero foil.

Get a piece of balsa wood about
8cm long.

Draw the shape of a wing on
the ends of the piece of wood.

Make the top curved and make
the back end thin.

USE SAND PAPER FOLDED
OVER A PIECE OF WOOD.

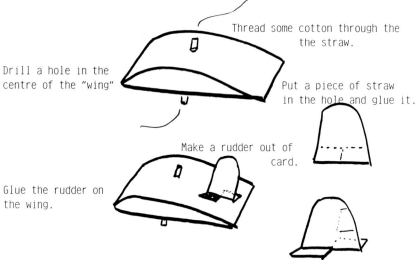

Your piece of wing should look like this.

Thread some cotton through the
the straw.

Drill a hole in the
centre of the "wing"

Put a piece of straw
in the hole and glue it.

Make a rudder out of
card.

Glue the rudder on
the wing.

Make the rudder like this.

BLOW AT THE WING   use a hair-dryer if you like...or just BLOW.

What did you expect to happen?   What really did happen?

Experiment 6.The "Magic" Cotton Reel

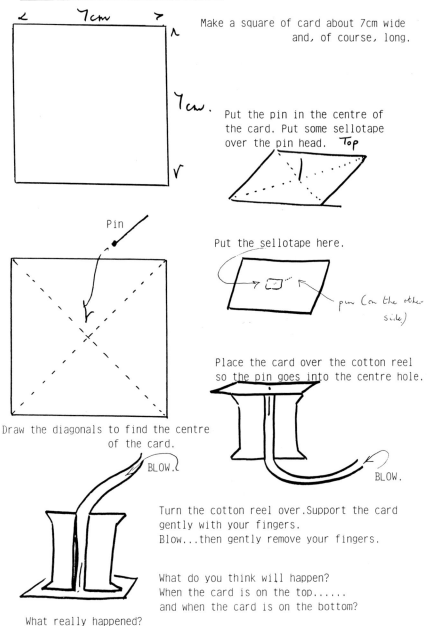

Make a square of card about 7cm wide
and, of course, long.

Put the pin in the centre of
the card. Put some sellotape
over the pin head. Top

Put the sellotape here.

pin (on the other side)

Place the card over the cotton reel
so the pin goes into the centre hole.

Pin

Draw the diagonals to find the centre
of the card.

BLOW.

BLOW.

Turn the cotton reel over.Support the card
gently with your fingers.
Blow...then gently remove your fingers.

What do you think will happen?
When the card is on the top......
and when the card is on the bottom?

What really happened?

DID the AUSTRALIAN ABORIGINES MAKE
the FIRST AEROFOIL?

The Boomerang is a very clever
weapon.
When you throw it,it comes back
to you.

Boomerangs are brilliantly made.
Not only are they bent in a very strange shape,the top surface is
curved like an aeroplane's wing.....an aerofoil!!!!

More than that,each end of the boomerang is tilted up...like an
aeroplane's wing when it takes off.

It's almost impossible to make a boomerang....for us that is!!!!
HOWEVER, it is possible to make a cardboard boomerang which should
work quite well.

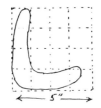

←— 5″ —→

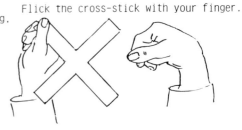

Flick the boomerang with a pencil.

You can make a cardboard   Flick the cross-stick with your finger.
  Cross-stick boomerang.

↑
↓ 1″

←——   8½″ —→

DID THE ANCIENT EGYPTIANS MAKE THE FIRST GLIDER?

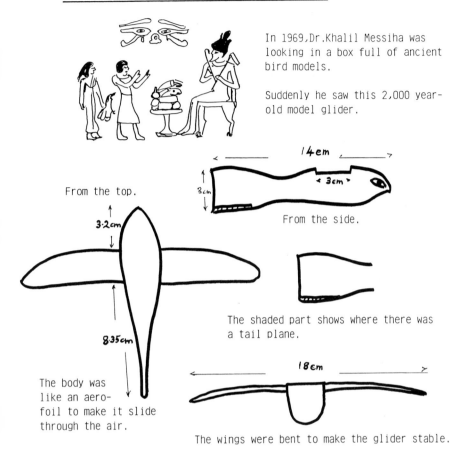

In 1969,Dr.Khalil Messiha was looking in a box full of ancient bird models.

Suddenly he saw this 2,000 year-old model glider.

14em

3cm

3cm

From the top.

From the side.

3·2cm

The shaded part shows where there was a tail plane.

8.35cm

18em

The body was like an aero-foil to make it slide through the air.

The wings were bent to make the glider stable.

Do you think you could make this ancient glider out of balsa wood.

SEE IF IT REALLY FLIES!!!!

MAKE A CHINESE KITE.

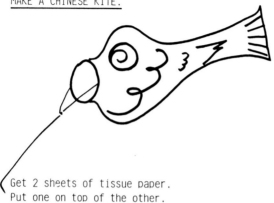

Get 2 sheets of tissue paper.
Put one on top of the other.

Draw a DRAGON Or a FISH Or a SNAKE Or a BIRD.....or anything!!!!

Cut out the Dragon.

Make a circle of
thin wire.

Glue the wire
into the mouth   of the dragon.

Glue the 2 sheets together...
ONLY round   the edges.

Tie some thin string on to the mouth. Do it round the wire.

round the wire
to make it strong

EVERYONE CAN MAKE A DIFFERENT KIND OF KITE.

Conclusion

The key questions for teachers raised by this chapter seem to be concerned with:

1 What support do we offer for developing skills and concepts through the medium of a second language? Is the activity as visual as it could be? Can pupils grasp what is happening and make their own inferences based on this without necessarily understanding what the teacher is saying?
2 Is the sole medium of input English, or are the mother tongues of bilingual children used? Is there bilingual support available from support staff, mainstream teachers, other pupils?
3 Developing an idea, interpreting information or an activity: what opportunities are provided for doing this for children whose facility in the medium of instruction is limited?
4 Use of passive voice: when do we introduce this, are we aware of the complexities of this verb form?
5 What styles, audiences and purposes are pupils required to write in and for? Do we make these clear to pupils and provide them with examples?
6 What form does the teacher's language take, and can pupils relate to this?
7 What are the teachers' attitudes to the pupils as learners through the medium of the second language?

During the past few years, an increasing number of texts have come from various sources about strategies for supporting bilingual pupils across the curriculum, and some of this work focuses on the science curriculum in both primary and secondary schools. Suggestions have been made for supporting pupils' oracy and literacy skills and many strategies have application across the curriculum. Some of the sources of these are listed in Chapter 5.

It is my hope that increasing numbers of teachers will now provide scientific opportunities for pupils in primary schools, which have the joint aim of developing cognitive and linguistic skills and of looking more closely at the activities and tasks they have chosen, to ascertain whether or not they involve children in a variety of conceptual and linguistic experiences. We need to be sure that all children, but particularly bilingual children, can be supported so that they have an equal opportunity to participate in and gain from these experiences. Let's work towards a positive response to the phrase 'the language of science'.

Chapter 5

Planning Science Lessons with a Multicultural Dimension

Alan Peacock

Introduction

Whenever I discuss the idea of 'multicultural science' with teachers, it doesn't take long before they begin to confess that they are anxious about 'having a go', and a number of reasons for this anxiety crop up over and over again. They are typified by comments such as:

> 'I don't know anything about other ways of baking bread . . .'
> 'Sometimes we stereotype people without realising it. I need more background knowledge about . . .'
> 'But where can I get hold of some (cooking utensils/musical instruments/Indian clothing) for this kind of activity?'
> 'Are there any books on (Islamic chemistry/Japanese medicine/African technology)?'
> 'Who were these famous black scientists?'
> 'How do I make sure I'm taking account of all the different issues in my lesson planning?'

These concerns fall roughly into three main categories, namely the need for (i) background information for the teacher, (ii) materials and resources for use by children, and (iii) effective planning of a multicultural dimension in science activities. This chapter will deal with each of these in turn, and will aim to point teachers in the direction of resources and methods available, rather than prescribe very specifically how to teach. In this area, more perhaps than in any other area of the primary curriculum, confidence is essential, and can only be acquired by gradually building up a range of techniques and materials which the individual owns and is happy with.

Sources of background information for teachers

Rather than trying to summarise the ideas in a wide range of materials, the list below contains titles of valuable background sources and where to obtain them. The key indicates the main focus of the text: all are science-oriented, or have sections on science.

KEY

Pr	Primary oriented
Sec	Secondary oriented, but with much of relevance to primary teachers
INSET	INSET focused
Act	Example activities described in detail
Pol	Discusses policies for multicultural science
Pla	Sections on planning multicultural activities in science
Bib	Good bibliography
pp	Number of pages

1 ILEA SCIENCE CENTRES (1987) *Science Teaching in a Multicultural Society. Book 1: Suggestions and Resources*, Sec, Act, Bib, pp 47, *Book2: Issues, Practices, Resources*. Sec, Act, Bib, pp 72. From Centre for World Development Education (CWDE) (01) 487 7410.

2 GILL, D. and LEVIDOW, L. (1987) *Anti-Racist Science Education*, Sec, Bib, Pol, pp 323. From Free Association Books (01) 609 5646.

3 SCIENCE FOR A MULTICULTURAL SOCIETY GROUP (1985) *Science Education for a Multicultural Society*. Sec, Pla, Act, Bib, pp118. From Leicestershire LEA (0533) 871388.

4 WATTS, S. (1983) 'Science Education for a Multicultural Society.' *Multicultural Teaching* Vol 1, (3) p. 3 Pol, Pla.

5 LINDSAY, L. (1985) *Racism, Science Education and the Politics of Food: an anti-racist approach to nutrition*. Sec, Act, Bib, pp 5. From ALTARF (01) 278 7856.

6 MANN, J., PEACOCK, A. and TOWNEND, C. (1988) *'Teaching science multiculturally in primary schools: recent initiatives in Leicestershire'*. Leicestershire Education, No. 9. Pla, Pr, Act, Pol, pp 4. From Leicestershire Centre for Multicultural Education (0533) 665451.

7 BUTTON, J. (1989) *The Primary School in a Changing World : A Handbook for Teachers*. INSET, Pr, Act, Pla, Bib, pp 106. From CWDE (01) 487 7410.

8 WILLIAMS, R. (1987) *Children and World Development*. Pr, INSET, pp 123. From UNICEF, UK/Richmond Publishing

9 KLEIN, G. (1984) 'Criteria for selecting classroom materials', in *Resources for Multicultural Education*. Pr, Pol, INSET, pp 3. From SCDC.

10 BIRMINGHAM DEVELOPMENT EDUCATION CENTRE (1986) *A Sense of School: Active Learning Approach to INSET*. Act, pp 56. From Birmingham DEC (021) 472 4231.

11 LEICESTERSHIRE LEA (1987) *An Aide-Memoire for Multicultural Education*. Pr, INSET, Pol, pp 43 from Leicestershire CME (0533) 665451.

12 SERTIMA, I. (1984) *Blacks in Science, Ancient and Modern*. Transaction Books USA. From Raddle Books, Leicester (0533) 624875.

13 ELKIN, J. and TRIGGS, P. (1985) *Childrens Books for a Multicultural Society*. Pr, Bib, pp 53. From 'Books for Keeps' (01) 852 4953.

14 BROOKING, C., FOSTER, M. and SMITH, S. (1981) *Teaching for Equality: Educational Resources on Race and Gender*. Pol, Bib, pp 118. From Runnymede Trust (01)387 8943.

15 YOUNG, B.L. (1979) *Teaching Primary Science* (Nigeria). Pr, Act, INSET, Pol, Pla, Bib, pp 217. From Longmans.

Materials and resources for use by children

The main source of materials for children will probably be your local authority's Multicultural Education Centre or Development Education Centre, or both: give them a ring first, or visit their library (resources centre). Alternatively, there are many local, national and international organisations which provide catalogues of publications. Examples of these are as follows.

International agencies:

UNESCO Catalogue of publications from UNESCO, 7 Place de Fontenoy, 75000 Paris, France.
UNICEF Office for Europe, Palias des Nations, CH1211, Geneva 10, Switzerland.

UK agencies

Centre for World Development Education, Regents College, Inner Circle Regents Park, London NW1 4NS.
Intermediate Technology Publications Ltd, 103/105 Southampton Row, London WC1B 4HH.

IPSE Directory of locally produced materials to promote science in primary schools, from ASE, College Lane, Hatfield, Herts AL10 9AA.

Local agencies

It is worth contacting your local Teachers Centre or College of Education which may have someone who specialises in this area. For example (in Birmingham), the African and Asian Resources Centre, Newman College, Weoley Park Road, Birmingham (021 472 7245).

Few commercially produced schemes of work for primary science have as yet tackled the question of multiculturalism: those that claim to, have not gone far beyond the use of black children in illustrations, whilst many opportunities have been overlooked. Much of the material for use by children has been produced locally by teachers, and is therefore difficult to obtain.

However, there are some useful materials, examples of which are:

WILLIAMS, I.W. (1984) *Third World Science : Resource Materials for Teachers.* From CWDE or School of Education, University College of North Wales, Bangor. (Worksheets in a wide range of activities, such as soapmaking, carrying loads, energy, etc)

OXFAM (1987) *The World in a Supermarket Bag* (Food activities for 7–11-year-olds) from Oxfam Youth and Education Dept (0865) 56777.

JONES, L. (1985) *Science and the Seeds of History.* Practical activities on farming, seeds, food tests, etc., with antiracist dimension. From Les Jones, Birley High School/Manchester Education Department.

STOLLAR, H. (1985) *Water Technology from around the World.* Worksheets on machines for moving water. From Waltham Forest Teachers Centre (01) 521 3311.

BATESON, P. and SHEPHERD, T. (1988) *The Water Game.* A topic-based computer simulation. From CWDE.

A wide range of such materials can be found in the Council for World Development Education catalogue 1989, free from CWDE.

Finally, many excellent ideas for multicultural science activities can be found in primary science schemes from other countries. Although these may not seem to be easy to obtain, many are published by international publishing houses with a UK base, and can therefore be purchased through their international divisions.

Good examples of useful schemes are:

BERLUTI, A. (1981a) *Beginning Science: A Course for Primary Schools in Kenya* (4 vols, upper primary). Macmillan Kenya, from Macmillan Publishers, 4 Little Essex Street., London WC2R 3LF

DOUGLASS, R. and FRASER-ABDER, P. (1984) *Primary Science for the Caribbean - A Process Approach*, Study workbooks 1-7. Heinemann Educational, London

DOUGLAS, O., WALKER, E. and AGARDE, K. (1988) *Science Revision and Tests for the Caribbean*, both covering primary age range, from Macmillan Caribbean, Houndmills, Basingstoke, Hants RG21 2XS.

Similar science schemes can also be obtained from other countries, e.g.

BHATTACHARYA, S. and RAMACHANDRAN, K. (1987) *Exploring Environment – Science* (3 vols, upper primary) from National Council for Educational Research and Training, Sri Aurobindo Marg, New Delhi 110016, India.

Planning a multicultural dimension into primary science

The shortage of materials specifically related to this area of concern suggests that science has probably been slower than most curriculum areas to respond to the needs of multicultural education. For this reason, a series of workshops evolved in Leicester for teachers in both multi-ethnic and all-white primary schools, which set out collaboratively to develop ideas, materials and ways of building-in to science a multicultural way of working.

As a consequence of these teachers' concerns, the planning checklist below evolved as a way of making sure that opportunities and links were not overlooked when planning schemes and activities. These concerns about planning are particularly acute as a result of national curriculum developments, and therefore the checklist attempts to take account of the skills, knowledge and understanding reflected in the attainment targets.

What does the national curriculum say about the multicultural dimension in primary science? Whilst the Statutory Orders do not refer to this as such, the final report of the Science Working Group (National Curriculum Science Working Group, 1988) on which the orders were based, contained six paragraphs on 'Science and Cultural Diversity' which stressed that:

1   Science must take account of the cultural diversity in school and society at large.
2   What we mean by 'science' may vary from culture to culture, no one culture has a monopoly of 'scientific' achievement.

3   The language of science can be complex, so teachers need to provide tangible examples which help children with these problems.
4   Pupils' own experiences, which should be the basis of much science learning, may be very different in relation to e.g. diet, health, energy, tools, utensils, etc., as a consequence of cultural differences. Thus teachers should not adopt a narrow view of what is the 'correct' diet, or the 'right' tool.
5   In designing tests and assessment activities, it is essential to avoid such ethnic or cultural bias.

This is very much in line with the points made in earlier chapters of this book. However, the statutory orders leave it up to individual teachers and schools to make whatever provision they believe to be appropriate, and therefore the checklist is intended to help teachers consider, at each stage of their planning, what opportunities can be taken to develop multicultural and antiracist perspectives.

The checklist (see p. 86) is in two parts. The first part, which occupies the centre of the spreadsheet, is a sequence of questions which takes teachers through the essential stages of planning, whilst the second part, in the boxes down each side, provides more detail relevant to some of the questions in part one. The remainder of this section quotes from the notes of one group of teachers who used the list to plan work on Food with 9–10-year-olds.

1   **Topic chosen?** Food.
2   **How many lessons/weeks?** One afternoon or its equivalent per week for one term, for the science component of the topic.
3   **Which investigative skills will children practise (AT1)?**
Particular emphasis will be given to:
   - exploring everyday experience, with increasing precision;
   - using an increasingly systematic approach;
   - moving from qualitative work to quantification of variables;
   - making increasingly precise measurements;
   - formulating and testing hypotheses;
   - searching for patterns in data.
4   **Which knowledge and understanding will they cover (ATs 2–17)?**
The work will cover aspects of:
   - feeding, growth and health (AT3)
   - similarities and differences in food plants and animals (AT4)
   - farming and waste disposal (AT5)

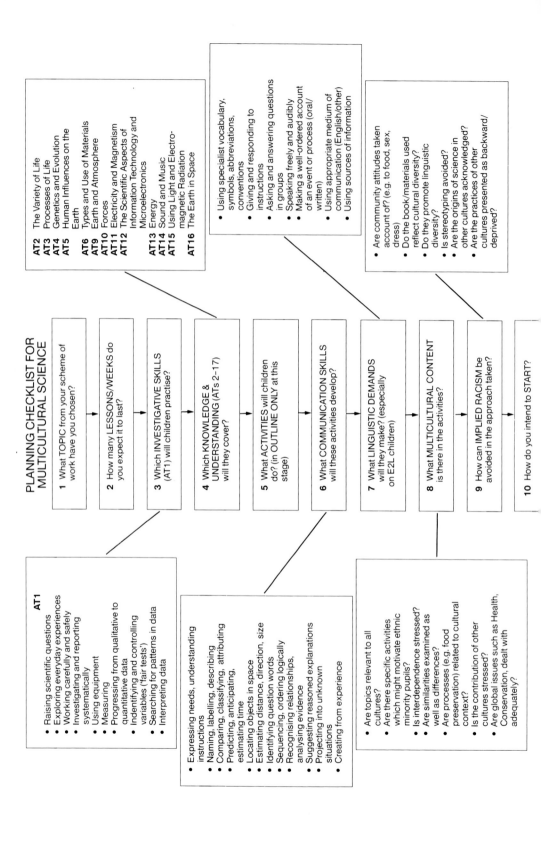

PLANNING CHECKLIST FOR MULTICULTURAL SCIENCE

1 What TOPIC from your scheme of work have you chosen?

2 How many LESSONS/WEEKS do you expect it to last?

3 Which INVESTIGATIVE SKILLS (AT1) will children practise?

4 Which KNOWLEDGE & UNDERSTANDING (ATs 2–17) will they cover?

5 What ACTIVITIES will children do? (in OUTLINE ONLY at this stage)

6 What COMMUNICATION SKILLS will these activities develop?

7 What LINGUISTIC DEMANDS will they make? (especially on E2L children)

8 What MULTICULTURAL CONTENT is there in the activities?

9 How can IMPLIED RACISM be avoided in the approach taken?

10 How do you intend to START?

AT2 The Variety of Life
AT3 Processes of Life
AT4 Genetics and Evolution
AT5 Human Influences on the Earth
AT6 Types and Use of Materials
AT9 Earth and Atmosphere
AT10 Forces
AT11 Electricity and Magnetism
AT12 The Scientific Aspects of Information Technology and Microelectronics
AT13 Energy
AT14 Sound and Music
AT15 Using Light and Electro-magnetic Radiation
AT16 The Earth in Space

- Using specialist vocabulary, symbols, abbreviations, conventions
- Giving and responding to instructions
- Asking and answering questions in groups
- Speaking freely and audibly
- Making a well-ordered account of an event or process (oral/written)
- Using appropriate medium of communication (English/other)
- Using sources of information

- Are community attitudes taken account of? (e.g. to food, sex, dress)
- Do the book/materials used reflect cultural diversity?
- Do they promote linguistic diversity?
- Is stereotyping avoided?
- Are the origins of science in other cultures acknowledged?
- Are the practices of other cultures presented as backward/deprived?

AT1

- Raising scientific questions
- Exploring everyday experiences
- Working carefully and safely
- Investigating and reporting systematically
- Using equipment
- Measuring
- Progressing from qualitative to quantitative data
- Identifying and controlling variables ('fair tests')
- Searching for patterns in data
- Interpreting data

- Expressing needs, understanding instructions
- Naming, labelling, describing
- Comparing, classifying, attributing
- Predicting, anticipating, estimating time
- Locating objects in space
- Estimating distance, direction, size
- Identifying question words
- Sequencing, ordering logically
- Recognising relationships, analysing evidence
- Suggesting reasoned explanations
- Projecting into unknown situations
- Creating from experience

- Are topics relevant to all cultures?
- Are there specific activities which might motivate ethnic minority pupils?
- Is interdependence stressed?
- Are similarities examined as well as differences?
- Are processes (e.g. food preservation) related to cultural context?
- Is the contribution of other cultures stressed?
- Are global issues such as Health, Conservation, dealt with adequately?

- changes which take place during cooking and preserving food (AT13)
- the use of different fuels for cooking (AT13)
- the design and use of different cooking utensils (Technology, AT1 and AT2)

5 What activities might children do?

Practical work will involve:

a) observing, measuring, describing a range of foods, their cooking and food value (e.g. fruits and vegetables)

b) measuring and describing changes in colour, size, shape through cooking (e.g. breads)

c) using, testing and designing cooking utensils of different materials (e.g. pans, woks, karahis, sufurias, pots)

d) growing seeds (e.g. fenugreek, coriander, moong beans)

For brevity, stages 6–10 of the checklist have been dealt with below in relation to only one of the activities (5b) above.

6 What communication skills will be developed?

- estimating and describing size, shape, weight, texture
- recognising and describing changes from unbaked to baked
- suggesting 'what will happen if' the baking process is changed, based on previous experience

7 What linguistic demands will be made?

- naming unfamiliar breads, in all appropriate languages
- following unfamiliar instructions for baking
- using new sources of information (recipes, shops, parents)

8 What is the multicultural content?

- learning what is the same and what is different about bread and baking in different cultures
- stressing processes which are common to all cultures (e.g. preserving fresh food)

9 How is implied racism avoided?

- by not stereotyping some tastes/foods as better/worse
- by using community languages for naming/labelling breads
- by discussing why some foods are unacceptable (e.g. animal fats to vegetarians)
- by avoiding books which only deal with 'our' kinds of bread and baking
- by questioning culture-specific notions (e.g. 'teatime')

10 How to start?

- bring a wide range of breads, and ask children to bring their 'favourite' bread for investigation

- name, label all breads (and list ingredients where possible), in appropriate languages
- observe changes taking place in toasting (size, colour, flexibility, weight, water content)
- bake two kinds of bread (leavened/unleavened) which children are familiar with
- measure changes taking place in baking (size, colour, texture, weight)
- work in multicultural/multilingual groups, where possible
- acknowledge that there are some kinds of bread/baking which you as teacher don't know about, and invite children to tell/show you about them
- suggest research into other ways of breadmaking

Much of the above is obvious. At the same time, very few teachers claim to work in this way, even where the materials required are readily available in homes and from corner shops. And many primary science magazines and articles overlook the multicultural possibilities which exist in most topics. If you have the experience and confidence in this approach you could encourage another teacher and class to work with you occasionally. The barrier of confidence, in both science and multicultural education, may be the biggest barrier to break down. Work through the planning checklist with another teacher: in that way you will generate so many more ideas. And when you have experienced the exhilaration of success, write and tell others about what you did.

Multicultural opportunities within the National Curriculum in Science

The programmes of study for key stages 1 and 2 specify the broad areas of skills, knowledge and understanding that schools are required by law to teach. At the same time, the Education Reform Act makes clear that schools have the responsibility for deciding how these skills and knowledge are taught. Thus the context of learning is very much a matter for individual schools and teachers.

This is stressed in the preamble to programmes of study for both key stages 1 and 2, in relation to Science in Everyday Life, where it is emphasised that 'children should use a variety of domestic and environmental contexts as starting points for learning science'. These contexts can clearly be the homes children live in; the clothes they wear; the food they eat; the festivals they celebrate; the toys and games they play with; the tools and utensils they use, or the work their parents do.

Most specifically at key stage 1, children are expected to undertake first-hand exploration of these objects and events, and to sort, group and describe them using all their senses, noting similarities and differences.

Within the knowledge and understanding attainment targets, many of the areas of study can be tackled multiculturally. For example, children can use *themselves* as a resource to consider similarities and differences, as discussed by Barbara Wyvill in Chapter 1. They can experience a wide range of *sounds* in their environment not only through use of musical instruments of different kinds, but also through the noises made in different places of work, or by different domestic objects. *Light and colour* are important dimensions in many festivals and celebrations, in flags and costumes of different nations (including football teams!), and in the many forms of jewellery and mirrors used in different cultures. *Keeping warm and keeping cool* assume different importance in different cultures, in clothing, refrigeration, cooking, heating and many other processes.

Many words connected with 'hotness' have different significance in different cultures, and terminology therefore has to be explored. (Ask a class of children to discuss the meanings of 'hot' and 'cool', to realise this!)

Related to this is the significance of sun, moon, day and night, and the *times* at which things happen. We tend to take all this for granted until we live in another part of the globe where these things look and feel very different. This also finds expression in the programme of study through relating changes in the *weather* to everyday activities.

In key stage 2, children are expected to investigate at least two different localities, and the ways in which *plants and animals* are suited to their location: and clearly, one of these could be a culturally different environment, since they are also encouraged to develop increasing independence in the use of sources.

The links between *health* and daily routine are a further area where cultural similarities and differences can offer wide scope for learning. One related issue is that of waste disposal and the attitudes of different cultures; what is waste to one may be a resource to another. Who does the disposing, and how?

Transmission and storage of information, whilst so often seen now as a matter of high technology, originated in number systems and languages of many other cultures, and it is important for children to recognise these origins. The same applies to work on *fuels*, their efficient use and where they come from. A teacher told me recently how one Asian girl's attitude to science had been transformed after they burned cowdung in the classroom, because it 'smelled like India!' The fact that we use vastly greater amounts of energy per head in Britain compared to many countries can be a source of much investigative work: do we need it? Can we save it? What does it do to the planet?

The forces which involve *movement* and are made use of in transport can also be the source of much comparative work. Can bikes, barges and mules be more sensible and efficient than planes and trucks in some contexts? What assumptions do we make about the need for speed, and are they justified? This can also underpin much of the work on electricity, its dangers and what uses we put it to.

All of these are over and above the usual topics such as food, ourselves, weather, etc., which crop up already in most schools and present wide-ranging opportunities for multicultural work, and which all have the dimension of communication, through practical collaboration and group discussion, which for many is at the heart of the multicultural ideal.

Chapter 6

Collaborating with Teachers to Produce New Materials

John Meadows

Introduction

Primary science is a complex mix of processes, concepts, attitudes and skills, with the pupils at the centre. As a primary school teacher for 15 years in inner city, multicultural schools, an advisory teacher for another two, and recently as a trainer of teachers and researcher, I have been interested mainly in the ideas that children hold, how they acquire these ideas, and the means which teachers can use to develop these ideas towards more scientific concepts.

In order to develop effective teaching materials for multicultural science education, it is essential to use all available expertise in a coherent way. Class teachers, researchers and INSET providers can and should cooperate to carry out this function, with a recognition of the important part each has to play. This chapter aims to give some insights into ways in which such collaborations have occurred and suggest further ideas for similar collaborations. The chapter thus describes a number of in-service courses, the background to them, and the ways in which various groups contributed to understanding and helping to develop children's learning of science concepts.

Background to the research and collaboration

There have been three main influences on the collaborative in-service training courses described later: first a small-scale research project on children's ideas about floating and sinking; next, a larger scheme involving London and Liverpool Universities, LEAs and schools; then a small project in schools in London's East End which involved teachers and student teachers.

In the small-scale research in two London primary schools, the children worked most frequently in groups of between two and six, though sometimes in classes of up to 25. They used a variety of common objects with transparent plastic water tanks. The objects included corks, pieces of various woods, expanded polystyrene blocks, chalk, wax crayons, candles, rubber stoppers, erasers, pencils, metal and plastic shapes, homemade models of rafts and boats, nails, screws and paperclips, small glass bottles, small logs, stones and gravel, etc.

Four questionnaires were used to find out the number and variety of reasons the children offered for the floating and sinking of the objects. In F/S 6 and 7, they were asked to fill in the questionnaires before trying out the objects in the water tanks; questionnaires F/S 1 and F/S 8 involved the use of three specified objects and the water tank. Two questionnaires (F/S 2 and F/S 3) were trialled and rejected as inappropriate for children at primary school level, and another two questionnaires (F/S 4 and F/S 5) had been eliminated in a previous pilot study.

The questionnaires could be completed, either by the child, or by the researcher if the child was unable to understand the format, or could not write or read fluently. Children in two schools in North and South London were tested. Altogether, 70 questionnaires were used in the South London school, and 140 in the North London school.

Some examples of outcomes from group interviews and questionnaires

SAMPLE 1 F/S1

With a group of children aged about 8 years, experimenting on three materials, expanded polystyrene, wood and metal, where they were encouraged to look at the weight and type of material, and predict before testing:

11 chose weight as the important factor
4 used their past experience, e.g. 'it will float because I've seen it float before'
2 quoted the type of material, and
1 said 'because it has a lot of wind in it'

SAMPLE 2 F/S8

With the same set of materials, but using a different questionnaire, where 13 possible reasons were itemised for the children to choose from:

the 6-year-olds gave an average of 4 reasons (ANOR = 1.3)
the 7-year-olds gave an average of 8 reasons (ANOR = 2.6) and
the 8-year-olds gave an average of 10 reasons (ANOR = 3.3)

(ANOR = average number of reasons = total reasons divided by number of items, in this questionnaire only – in others, the ANOR is the total number of *types of reason* offered by the children divided by the total number of children in the sample.)

SAMPLE 3 F/S6

With a group of 10 infant children aged 5 or 6, talking about ships, trees, logs of wood and swimming, using a diagrammatic questionnaire:

7 mentioned size as a factor
3 mentioned weight
3 mentioned hardness
1 said strength
1 said air
1 said the type of material, and
1 said the colour

ANOR = 1.7

Of these 5–6-year-old children, eight mentioned more than one reason as important. Many of the replies were consistent with the child's own logic, e.g. a tree will 'float' because 'it's big and heavy', while a piece of wood will 'sink' because 'it's small and fat' – from Nipa, a Bengali-speaking girl aged 5 years with good English. Another example from a Chinese-speaking girl, also aged 5 years, whose English was still very rudimentary, shows the earliest stage of thinking – a tree will float 'cos it's a tree', and a small piece of wood will float because 'it's wood' (Dentici *et al.*, 1985) although she also showed signs of progressing to the next stage when she said that a ship floated because 'it's big'.

SAMPLE 4 F/S6

Using the same questions as in sample 3, but with a group of twelve 9–10-year-olds, who could write their own answers, the results were quite different:

20 mentions of weight
7 of air in things

4 of the type of material and

3 of size

3 of relative weight (all from the same girl)

ANOR = 3.1

With the older children, weight has taken over from size as the major factor quoted for floating and sinking. Another significant difference is that
the younger children gave an average of 1.7 reasons (17 reasons from 10
children), while the older pupils gave an average of 3.1 (37 reasons from
12 children), almost twice as many as they younger children.

Analysis of results and conclusions

One immediate conclusion was that the type of questionnaire and activity used have an effect on the number of reasons offered by the child for
the floating or sinking of objects – the average number of reasons given
varied from 1.2 to 2.5 for different types of questionnaire.

A second conclusion is that age or stage of development is an important factor in the number of reasons offered.

The number of reasons offered for floating and sinking by children at different ages

Age range	Number of reasons		Total	Average
	North	South		
5–6	2	–	2	2
6–7	1.5	–	1.5	1.5
7–8	1.8	–	1.8	1.8
8–9	2.3	2.2	4.5	2.3
9–10	1.6	3.6	5.2	2.6
10–11	2.6	2.8	5.4	2.7

A third conclusion concerns consistent and inconsistent reasoning.
There appeared to be a gradual increase in consistency with age. In this
study, consistent was defined as an internal consistency of reasons
offered by the child: it does not imply that such reasoning is consistent
with experimental results and findings, or observations, nor consistent
with the accepted scientific explanations. It referred only to the children's
own framework of ideas, e.g. if a child always says 'heavy things sink and
light things float', this was considered consistent. If on the other hand,
another child says that light things sink and heavy things float, this was

also considered as consistent, even though it contradicted the evidence as much as the first statement.

Implications

This study described the development of children's concepts about materials and floating and sinking. There seemed to be definable stages in this development of children's ideas.

1 Earlier stages were characterised by an emphasis on size and weight of objects.
2 An intermediate stage was identified as corresponding to attempts to describe a single reason.
3 Later stages seem to involve an increase in the number and internal consistency of the responses, linked to the emphasis on weight and other reasons, such as type of material, hardness, size, previous experience, etc. However, the internal consistency of the children's theories about floating and sinking seems to decrease at a certain stage, as they strive to make links between their increasing experiences and their conceptual frameworks.

The development of ideas about the reasons for floating and sinking is not a regular progress towards a scientific understanding of the concept of density, but rather a series of forward, backward and sideways moves through a series of changing conceptual 'islands'. Each change can be encouraged by challenging the child's existing ideas through the provision of activities and experiences accompanied by questions and discussions.

The framing of questions depended very much on the replies the child gave to the first questions. From taped interviews with children, some useful questions were devised to follow up their initial responses:

Teacher: 'What do you think this log will do when you put it in (the water)?'
Child: 'Go down.'
T: 'Why do you think it will go down?'
C: 'It's big.'
T: 'What about big ships? Will they sink too?'
C: 'No, because they have air in.'

Teacher: 'Why do you think the rubber bung sank?' (red rubber bung with two holes in it)
Childrens possible answers and subsequent questions:
1   **C:** 'Because it's red' – **T:** 'Will this red marble sink too?'
2   **C:** 'Because it has holes' – **T:** 'How about this polystyrene block with holes in it?'
3   **C:** 'Because it's heavy' – **T:** 'Is it as heavy as the log?'
4   **C:** 'Because it's rubber' – **T:** 'Do you think all rubber things will sink? Can you find some more rubber objects to test?'
5   **C:** 'Because it's round' – **T:** 'Will this tennis ball sink, it's round isn't it?'
(**C** means child, **T** is teacher)

Although this approach may produce the required conflict in the child's thinking, it is very difficult for a teacher to do it in a busy classroom, with many other children also requiring attention. A solution to this is to have children working in groups around the water trays, and looking at a small selection of objects which they have to report on to the whole class later. The teacher can then start off the questioning in a similar manner, and encourage the children themselves to raise questions about the verbal reports.

Another problem which can arise with this type of questioning is that many children presume that the teacher has the right answer in her/his head, and the questions are just designed for the child to guess that answer. Children need to be reassured that the answers they give are respected and valued as an important part of the continuous process of learning. 'Practical work is not enough on its own . . . children need time to think and talk through.' (Driver 1981).

A further problem for children with a poor grasp of the dominant language is that they may be unable to join in with such discussions, unless there are sufficient numbers of them to be able to discuss things in their home language, or with a teacher who understands this language as well as the science which the pupils are discussing. However, one could adopt an alternative viewpoint on this issue and regard the science activities and dicussions as a way to enhance the language development of such children. For example, in the dialogue between teacher and pupil concerning a log of wood (above), the child's response 'go down' was developed by the teacher into the more scientific term 'sink'.

It would be unfortunate if pupils with English as a second language were deprived of experiences in science which might easily help both their understanding of science and of English language. An example of such links between science and language happened with an 8-year-old

Turkish girl, who had been in England for only two weeks. She was working with a group of other pupils on electricity, and was able to test and sort materials into conductors and insulators, using a simple bulb, battery and wire circuit. This activity allowed her to practise her very rudimentary English words and phrases in a context where she was learning new science ideas on equal terms with the other pupils, and also allowed her to begin to integrate socially with her peers.

Research with the SPACE project (in collaboration with Jonathon Usborne and Maureen Smith)

SPACE (Science Processes and Concept Exploration) is a classroom-based action research project which attempts to explore and describe the ideas and understandings primary school children have in a number of areas of science. It also aims to discover how these ideas can be affected by classroom activities and experiences, developed by cooperation between teachers and researchers, based on the pupils ideas. The assumption is that children's ideas are developed through their experiences, and that to teach scientific concepts, it is necessary to know what current ideas and misconceptions children hold, then to challenge these constructively in order to effect changes.

The classroom work can be categorised into three stages:

(a) exploration of current ideas,
(b) interventions aimed at challenging unscientific concepts,
(c) examination of changes in children's understandings.

Stages (a) and (c) were carried out by individual or group interviews with children, and by written and diagrammatic questionnaires. Stage (b) occurred in the normal classroom, with children working in their usual manner, though often with a researcher helping the class teacher.

There are two main centres for the project, one at Liverpool University, the other at King's College, London. The project is funded by the Nuffield Foundation and is supported by Local Education Authorities. Published results have begun to be produced from the early stages in 1989.

The areas which have been studied are:

in London schools: electricity and light
in Liverpool schools: evaporation/condensation
                       changes in non-living materials
                       forces and their effects on movement

growth
living things, sensitivity to their environment
sound

Several publications exist at the time of going to press (Osborne et al., 1990; Russell and Watt, 1990a, b; Watt and Russell, 1990)

Naturally, since it is dependent on cooperation between teachers, researchers and local authority advisory teachers (with an INSET responsibility), the project has developed in different ways at each centre and in each local authority.

This outline deals with some work undertaken in London on children's ideas about light.

A. Exploration stage

A pilot study was carried out to explore children's ideas about a variety of sources of light, including torches, candles and mirrors. Three main areas to focus on were chosen from the results of the pilot study: sources, vision and representations of light. Teachers and researchers met to discuss the actual questions to be used in interviews and questionnaires, the concepts they considered it important for pupils to begin to grasp, and other practical details. Decisions were then made by teachers and researchers about the questions and activities to be used in the main project. These decisions were based on such criteria as:

1   How clear and unambiguous the questions were for children to understand.
2   How much the answers from the pilot study revealed about the children's ideas.
3   How easy the activities were to carry out in the normal classroom, by children usually working in cooperative groups.
4   How much equipment was needed for the activities – normally, only resources that would be found in primary classrooms were considered for use in the project, though some materials were supplied to schools to make it easier for teachers to carry out the work within the time available, rather than having to await the arrival of equipment orders.

B. Intervention stage

Four main types of intervention were used:

1 Torch and three or four mirrors – getting the light from a powerful torch to reflect off each mirror onto the next, around the top of a table.

2 Torch and shadows – predicting and testing what happens to the shadow if torch, object or screen are moved in various ways.

3 Light boxes – a box (such as a cereal packet) with small holes in the sides, a viewing hole at one end and a mirror taped to the inside at the other end. Children were asked to predict and test what happened to the light when the torch was shone into one of the holes, either straight across the box, or onto the mirror in the box.

4 Discussing and answering questions about a set of drawings showing scenes with light:
   (i)   cats eyes at night,
   (ii) a child with a birthday cake with lighted candles,
   (iii) a night-time street scene with pedestrian, car with headlights on and street light,
   (iv) dark room with door ajar and a narrow beam of light entering from this door,
   (v)   a child reading a book with the help of a desk lamp.

These activities were again discussed and tried out in meetings with teachers and researchers before being introduced to the pupils in their classrooms.

C. Changes in children's ideas

Changes in children's understandings were determined by the use of a set of questions similar to that used in the exploration stage of the project. Some of the results are described below.

At first, light was rarely represented in children's drawings. After the intervention activities, many children began to use lines, often with arrows showing direction, to represent light. Other less frequent representations included dotted lines, blobs of light on mirrors or sources, or shading to show a 'sea of light'.

Many children think of light coming from places such as windows, mirrors and ceilings, rather than from the original source of the sun or light bulbs. The questioning in part determined the kinds of responses children gave about light sources, although many children still considered the moon as a light source. Reflection of light was frequently misunderstood – many children used the term 'reflect' to mean light travelling rather than 'bouncing off' a surface, as in 'light reflects to the mirror', rather than 'light reflects from the mirror'. In the light of the points made in Chapter 4, it is reasonable to suppose that children with English as a second language would have even more difficulty in expressing such ideas, which demand an accurate use of language.

Very few children had a scientific understanding of vision as the passage of light from a source to an object to the eye. After the intervention activities, many children indicated links between eyes and object, some showed links between light sources and object, others showed dual links between light source, object and eyes. More frequent was the idea that vision involves an 'active eye', often indicated by an arrow coming *from* the eye *towards* the object being looked at. Another important change was that many more children indicated the need for light in order to be able to see.

Few children expressed their ideas about vision in a consistent manner – most of the ideas were dependent on the particular context used, so that, for example, a child might display one response when asked about seeing a candle, but a different response when thinking about seeing a clock.

The next stage of this research project is expected to involve further collaborations with teachers, looking at children's ideas in other areas of primary science, working together to develop more activities and experiences for pupils, and spreading the ideas gathered so far through INSET courses, publications and conferences.

Collaborative research with teachers and student teachers

This project arose out of the research done in a primary school in Islington, described earlier. One was an investigation of the ways in which children with English as a second language cope with concept development in science.

Working with English, Bengali and Chinese-speaking children led to the proposal of a hypothesis: that there are stages through which most children travel on the way to acquiring a concept of density of materials. The identification of these stages was a major concern of the early work on floating and sinking.

The proposed stages are identified by:
(a) the *number* of reasons children offer for the floating and sinking of objects,
(b) by the *types* of reasons, and
(c) by the *consistency* of the reasoning.

Results have been analysed in these three ways, as well as by age and home language of the child. As already pointed out, results are not always straightforward, since the type of questionnaire can have an effect upon any one of the outcomes.

The second phase of the project involved some work, again on floating and sinking, with groups of children at two schools, in Hackney and in Brixton. The third phase, outlined here, was based on the principle that class teachers should be doing research with children they know – i.e. 'the teacher as researcher'. Tower Hamlets was chosen for the project because of the interest of the teachers' centre warden and advisory teachers in primary science over the years, because of the presence of large numbers of ESL children in the schools, and because a number of Tower Hamlets primary schools have reached an advanced stage in the development of science teaching.

One of the main aims of the project was to devise teaching strategies and materials to help teachers to do good science work, in other areas of primary science, with the whole range of children in their schools. Progression was an important factor in the scheme – not age-related, but with reference to any recognisable stages in the development of concepts (important ideas) and process skills.

The implications for the teachers were that they would need to know:

1   How to recognise a child's stage and future needs,
2   How to use the materials with children at different stages in the same class.
3   How to monitor and evaluate the progress of children.

Structuring the Activities

This was done by:
1   Providing a worksheet before the practical work, to explore children's ideas and predictions.
2   Discussing with the children the predictions they made.
3   Carrying out specific activities.
4   Discussing the results and children's ideas about the meaning of these.
5   Using a worksheet or interview after activities – with drawing and writing, to determine what changes may have occurred in children's understanding.

The emphasis throughout was on the children expressing their own thoughts, not on getting standardised 'right answers'. The worksheets are not marked right or wrong, but are to indicate the understandings of the children. It can be difficult for some children (and some teachers too) to realise that this kind of work demands their active participation as partners in the learning process, and that a lot of trust is required by both in order to achieve meaningful results.

Students from a B.Ed course were involved in the project, in the preparation of activities and questions for use in interviews, in working with pupils in classes alongside teachers, and in analysing the results of their own work with their colleagues who had visited other schools and classes. Six schools were visited by 18 students, who worked on a number of different areas of science, including Paper (to link with a project on materials already in progress), Electricity (linking with the students' own work in this area) and Light (to pursue some ideas arising from the SPACE project).

Although the project did encounter certain difficulties and was complicated to organise, it did have a number of positive results:

1   It gave the students an insight into the research process.
2   It helped them to understand the problems faced by a classroom teacher who wishes to carry out science activities with groups, and some ways of solving these problems.
3   It gave them an opportunity to work with children from a variety of cultural backgrounds, without being judged themselves, as they would be on their own teaching practices.
4   It helped the classroom teachers by giving them extra 'hands' in their classrooms, and gave them some extra ideas about activities and evaluations of children's learning.

Ideas for future collaborations

Possible strategies for future work with teachers include:

1   A joint research project, using schools in New York which have large numbers of Hispanic-speaking pupils, along the lines of the floating and sinking project already described, though maybe with a different science focus. Some US administrators and science coordinators have been approached about this and some interest has been shown. It is likely that such a project will occur in the near future.
2   A Primary Science summer school for visiting American teachers. Teachers from Tower Hamlets might become involved in the tutoring of the course. This might take the form of presenting seminar papers

on the research or classroom science teaching. The American teachers might also visit some of the Tower Hamlets primary schools to see science teaching in action.

3   Visits by English teachers to the United States to see how science and second language issues are dealt with. Schemes involving such visits already take place in other parts of London.

4   Developing strategies for overcoming problems about language, which might include:

(a)   using interpreters, from the same class, school or family;

(b)   grouping children who speak the same language together for the science activities;

(c)   vocabulary exercises, using practical activities, materials, pictures and diagrams – labelling items used, etc.,

(d)   taping and analysing conversations, looking at common misconceptions, analysing teachers' sentence constructions and children's own use of grammar, examining questioning.

Inservice training course

INSET sessions have been run in a number of general-purpose teacher centres in Inner London. Each INSET course covered five sessions and was advertised in the teachers' centre termly booklet. These advertisements stressed the active, investigatory nature of science, but also mentioned the need to take account of the proposals of the National Curriculum Working Group on Science. A further focus was on the need for teachers to evaluate the learning which was taking place, and ways in which this learning could be assessed. There was an expectation that teachers would be involved in trialling materials and feeding back their results into group discussions.

The five sessions dealt with the five main themes of the National Curriculum (Living Things, Materials, Forces, Energy, Earth and Space) and began with general ideas about action research and the methods to be used, including practical investigations, discussion, reporting, recording and evaluating classroom strategies.

Although the normal pattern of the course was for a one and a half hour session each week for the five weeks, one course was arranged with fortnightly sessions (in the event, this arrangement did not produce good results, perhaps because the impetus was not maintained regularly and many teachers did not attend for the whole course).

Other factors affecting the courses included the time of year in which they were run; summer term is not particularly useful, since many teachers have commitments to school journeys, sports days, parents evenings, etc. The time near Christmas is often equally busy for teachers in schools, with concerts, plays, special displays to organise, etc.

The obvious problem with teachers trying out such activities in their own classrooms each week is that primary teachers tend to plan topics to last for a number of weeks, not to introduce new material each week. However some of the participating teachers were able to use some of the worksheets/questionnaires, as they fitted with the topics they were already engaged on, whilst other materials were used in response to initial INSET activities and continued with in the classrooms during the whole course.

Some examples of questionnaires and worksheets devised and used during the INSET courses follow here.

Night and Day

Name:_____ How old are you? _____

1. Draw two pictures of the same place, one in daylight, the other at night. Use white and black paper.
2. How do we see at night?
3. What happens to sunlight at night?
4. How do the sun, moon and earth look from outer space? Draw them and show how they move.
5. Draw some things that give out light.
6. How do you think an electric light works?

Light 1
Use a mirror and a torch, with a partner. Shine the torch light onto the mirror, from behind your partner's head, so that they can see the light. How do they see it?
Finish the picture showing what happens to the light from the torch.
[A diagram is used here, showing a child's face, a torch behind her/his head and a mirror in front.]
What happens to the light when it reaches the mirror?
Is light from the torch going towards the face, or away from it?
What else could you say about this experiment?

Light 2
Look at a candle, burning in a sand tray. Draw it, showing the flame and the light. How far does the light go?
Look at the candle light in a mirror. What happens to the light at the mirror?
Finish this drawing to show how the child sees the light from the candle. [A diagram is used, showing the candle alight and a child looking at it.]

Cars on slopes
Find a way of making a smooth slope, and roll some cars down it.
Which sort of car travels best?
How far do the cars go, once they reach the floor?
Draw a picture showing how you did the tests.
Why do some cars go better than others?
How could you test if your explanation is correct?

Gravity
What do you think gravity does?
Why does a stone fall back to earth after you throw it up?
How can birds stay up in the air?
How do you think aircraft can stay up in the air?
Try making parachutes from paper, plastic or material. Which is the best sort of parachute?
Draw your parachute being tested, and measure some of its parts.

Long Jump
Which two children do you think can do the longest jumps?
Why do you think that?
How would you test this?
Try to measure these things and fill in your results here.
Name:_____ Height:_____
Leg length:_____ Length of Jump:_____
Does the person with the longest legs jump best?
Does the tallest person jump the best?
What else could be a reason for jumping far?

Conclusions and implications

The 'long jump' questions were produced by collaborations after a session on 'Ourselves', and during a week in which many of the teachers had been trying out some of the ideas generated. An additional aim was to attempt to evaluate how well pupils were able to use the process skills of prediction, examining, variables and drawing conclusions. This session took place in a summer term during good weather, when many teachers were doing athletics activities with their classes. Much of the discussion centred on the exact wording of the questions, so that children were encouraged to think scientifically and to record such thinking. Teachers often express their worries about the recording of scientific investigations. The activities themselves may work very well, children may be learning and enjoying the work, but when they are asked to record it, they find it difficult and the results are disappointing. The purpose of many of the worksheets and questionnaires devised and discussed in these INSET courses was to enable children to record not only the methods and results of investigations, but also the decisions they made and the reasons behind such decisions.

'Cars on slopes' was one of the most successful to date, since it was tried out by the teachers during one of the early sessions, before they used it in their classrooms – age ranges of pupils included nursery (age 4–5 years) up to third year Junior (age 9–10 years). Drawings and writing were brought to subsequent sessions, as well as photographs of children doing the various activities. There was enormous enthusiasm from one group of teachers to discuss their own pupils' responses; compare them with those of other teachers; reflect upon the stages of development which seemed to be characteristic of pupils at certain ages, the process skills the children were learning, and the positive attitudes of pupils to these types of practical activities. The positive attitudes of children of all ages towards practical science work was remarked upon frequently, particularly where the pupils were required to make some decisions about the design or methods of measurement, etc, as opposed to the more passive role normally experienced by pupils. Many of these teachers were at first reluctant to allow much decision-making to be done by the pupils, perhaps because they themselves lacked either the knowledge or the confidence to be able to steer their pupils into productive lines of enquiry.

Multicultural issues arising from INSET sessions

Smell tests

Often herbs and spices, or crisps of different flavours are used in such tests. One needs to be sensitive to the use of beef and bacon flavoured crisps if pupils from certain religious and cultural backgrounds are present in the group.

The word 'curry' can become a derogatory expression among some pupils. Science activities can be developed into a way of combatting racism by examining the ingredients of curry powders more closely, e.g. smell, taste, colour, their uses in specific dishes, areas of world where particular spices originate. Topics on senses, taste and smell can lead on to studies of traditional dishes which use different kinds of spices, e.g. cardamoms, ginger, turmeric, chili, coriander, or different amounts, e.g. tandoori, madras, or vindaloo dishes.

Grouping of pupils for investigations

Situations sometimes arise in schools where children are reluctant to work with others of a different race, gender, colour, etc. Science activities can be used in some cases to overcome such prejudices. Pairs of pupils can, for certain activities, be chosen by the teacher, not always by children themselves (decisions need to be shared, sometimes teacher sometimes pupil; the teacher, after all, has the responsibility for the hidden as well as the overt curriculum). An example might occur during an electricity workshop, where each pupil is given one bulb, one battery and one wire to start investigations on ways of lighting up the bulb – cooperation is then necessary in order to progress to investigations on lighting the bulb with one battery, examining effect of two batteries on one bulb, or two bulbs from one battery, etc.

Sensitive teachers can use this opportunity to pair up children in certain ways, e.g. boy with girl, English with Punjabi, or any other way that is considered important in the particular situation. The enthusiasm of most pupils for the activity/investigation itself will often outweigh any qualms they may have about such cooperation, as may the desire to succeed in mastering some skill or new situation.

Light investigations

Investigations on light and vision may lead to discussions about lights used in a number of religious and cultural festivals, e.g. Diwali, the Hindu festival of light, where pujas (small clay and oil or wax lanterns) are used, Christmas, the Christian festival where fir trees are decorated with lights, or Easter, where an Easter candle burns as a symbol of new life.

Touch tests

Muslim pupils may have reservations about exposing certain parts of their bodies. One of my American students on a summer school INSET course assured the class that her Muslim pupils would not be allowed to carry out touch tests on their feet, a taboo I had never heard of before. One danger here is that of stereotyping pupils. We need to be aware that there are many differences between people within most cultures: there is as much diversity of attitude and practice within Jewish, Muslim or other groups as there is within the Christian culture with which we are most familiar.

PART II

Science for All? Lessons from Home and Abroad

Chapter 7

Science for All? Antiracism, Science and the Primary School

Barry Troyna and Steve Farrow

Anti-racism: a 'loony tune'?

It is now customary, almost *de rigeur* to denounce antiracist education. The caricatured and malevolent reconstruction of events in Brent, Haringey, Dewsbury and Burnage High School has ensured that antiracist education is assigned demoniac properties. It is characterised as a child of the 'loony left' and especially of those socialist local education authorities described by Kenneth Baker as 'apostles of mediocrity and bigots of indoctrination' (7 October 1987). What is most insidious in this trend, however, is the tendency to contrast antiracist education with 'real education', a sleight of hand neatly deployed by Margaret Thatcher at the Conservative party's annual conference in 1987. Then, it will be recalled, she told delegates: 'Children who need to be able to count and multiply are learning antiracist mathematics – whatever that may be' (9 October 1987). The 'anti-antiracist' crowd, then, is expanding at an inexorable rate. Nor are its constitutents drawn exclusively from the right – although that is where its most influential and assertive exponents tend to be (Oldman, 1987). No, the 'anti-antiracist' crowd also includes members who are committed to cultural pluralism and 'prejudice reduction' but who find antiracism too 'political, confrontational, accusatory and guilt-inducing' (Lynch, 1987, p.x). These 'new multiculturalists' as Richard Hatcher (1987) calls them, echo Tory critiques of antiracism as 'propaganda' and parody its aims and approaches (Parekh, 1986, for instance).

Against this bleak background it may seem unrealistic to expect antiracism to assume either a profound or pervasive influence on the way science teaching is conceived and implemented in primary schools. The move towards centralisation in conjunction with the introduction of attainment testing represents the restoration of conservative principles and practices in education. The imposition of this ideological framework on education will be of immense significance, and will impede the antiracist task even more. But even in this depressing scenario it is possible to catch a glimmer of light. To begin with, equality of opportunity continues to be advanced as an organising principle of the education system. Baker makes explicit reference to it, for instance, in the consultation document on the National Curriculum (National Curriculum Science Working Group, 1987, p.4). It is our contention, shared by teachers and others throughout the country, that by appealing to this fundamental tenet we can legitimate activity developed from antiracist and antisexist perspectives. Put another way, it is quite plausible to insist that antiracist and antisexist forms of education are crucial in the struggle for the realisation of equality of opportunity in education. Secondly, whilst acknowledging the straitjacket effect of the National Curriculum on what is taught, we follow Tony Jeffs in his claim that: 'Despondency need not be the order of the day' (1988, p.47). Why? Well, he puts it like this:

> It is essential not to overestimate the importance of the curriculum and the timetable, since in relation to matters of beliefs, attitude and values the wider context of the school organisation and the pattern of classroom control are far more influential than the content of lessons. (Jeffs, 1988, p.47)

The thrust of this chapter, then, will be concerned with outlining the principles which might underpin the organisational, administrative and pedagogic strategies of antiracist education. We hope to provide what might be termed the 'Zanussi' theory: namely, the 'appliance' of antiracist principles to science rather than substantive examples of what an antiracist science curriculum in primary schools might look like.

Our starting point must be, however, with the current status of science teaching in primary education. From there we will look briefly at what research has to tell us about how teachers of science conceive and respond to antiracist education. Third, we will look at recent policy pronouncements relating to science teaching and antiracist education. These three areas provide a contextual background to the main task in hand; that is, to present the set of principles and concerns which unite those committed to the development and implementation of antiracist education.

Science education, 'race', primary schools and teachers

No one can doubt the burgeoning growth of science education in primary schools. In recent years this has been expressed in the form of various curriculum initiatives at local, regional and national level geared towards the promotion and legitimation of science teaching in primary education. Nonetheless, whilst there are few schools, if any, that would not include science as a major component of their curriculum, it is only with the 1988 Education Reform Act that it has been assigned status as a cornerstone of primary education. There are, perhaps, two reasons for this belated development. The first concerns the nature of the curriculum initiatives; the second is a function of the scientific background, professional education and orientation of the primary school teacher. Of course, these two considerations are interdependent; after all, the diffusion of a primary science policy – as with any other – depends upon the conviction of the teachers charged with its implementation.

In general terms, the curriculum initiatives of the 1960s and '70s (e.g. *Nuffield Junior Science; Science 5–13*) have had a low uptake in schools (Schools Council, 1979) and a minimal impact on the underlying principles of curriculum planning (Plimmer, 1981; Kerr and Engel, 1980). One of the more plausible explanations for this focuses on the failure of the innovators to convince their non-specialist colleagues of the value and efficacy of the initiatives (Plimmer, 1981). In this sense, then, the procedure adopted for the promotion and implementation of these innovative science materials and techniques contravened some of the most basic principles governing curriculum innovation. But the failure of these innovators to effect more than a patchy and limited change is not the whole story.

Don Plimmer argues convincingly that it is the distinguishing characteristics of the primary school teaching profession which militate most strongly against the integration of science into their habitual practices. He maintains that the education system continues to deliver primary teachers who are self-confessed non-specialists. Within this broad context there has been a range of mutually supporting trends which have converged and account for the current erratic profile of science in primary education. For example:

1   Few initial teacher education courses have until very recently contained a compulsory science element.
2   Primary school teachers have often followed 'humanities'-based courses in secondary school. In consequence, the population from which primary teachers tend to be recruited has, therefore, already

largely rejected science as a study area in its own education.

3   Science has an 'inhuman' image. It is popularly conceived as standing against humanities. After all, scientists have evolved the means of human destruction and have caused (but can no longer control) the pollution of the planet.

4   The primary teaching force continues to be dominated, in quantitative terms, by women. Female exclusion from science subjects, when these become optional in the secondary school, obviously encourages these teachers to see themselves as non-specialists.

Clearly these are pertinent and still potentially forceful inhibitors of change. But they should not be allowed to deflect attention from the emerging presence of science in the primary curriculum. As we have said, the enactment of the Education Act (1988) will see science assume even higher priority in the planning of primary education. Against this background, then, it is appropriate to consider two things. First, how likely is it that the content, orientation and purpose of science teaching in the primary school will be suffused by antiracist perspectives? Second, given that the potential for 'bottom up', grassroots initiatives to impact on the curriculum will be constrained by current moves towards centralisation, we need to ask: to what extent will the development of antiracist science teaching be expedited by central policy and guidance?

On the face of it, the prospects for integrating antiracist concerns into primary school science are not encouraging. Indeed, all the relevant research indicates that specialist science teachers, on the one hand, and primary school teachers, on the other, are the two constituent professional groups most resistant to the arguments of antiracist education. Study after study has shown, for instance, that science teachers (in secondary schools) are the least innovatory in their teaching and most dismissive of equal opportunities policies and practices (Kelly *et al.*, 1985; Pratt, 1985). More specifically, Troyna and Ball's study of teachers in 'Milltown' schools revealed that science teachers were far less likely than their colleagues in arts or creative arts departments and faculties to say that they encouraged multicultural – never mind antiracist – education, in the development of their department's work (Troyna and Ball, 1987). Nor, if the research of Sheila and Tony Turner is to be believed, is this likely to change dramatically in the future. Their study of the status of multicultural education in the initial education of science teachers throughout the country showed that the commitment was both patchy and incidental. Although the tutors in their survey were not, by and large, unconvinced by the educational significance of multicultural education, many hesitated to give priority to this theme in discussions about their subject (Turner and Turner, 1987).

On the other hand, multicultural education (in contrast to antiracist conceptions of reform) is in the ascendancy in primary schools, especially those in multi-ethnic settings. Here, however, a particular version of mutlticulturalism prevails. Troyna and Ball's study of schools in 'Milltown' indicated that policies and practices in local primary schools centred around what Troyna (1984) termed the 'three Ss' approach: Saris, Samosas and Steel Bands. In other words, there is an emphasis on the presentation of exotic minority group lifestyle in the curriculum and associated materials and resources. This interpretation is fostered in the belief that by introducing white pupils to different cultures and lifestyles, racist and stereotypical beliefs will be dislodged. Of course, this assumption is erroneous and evidence exists to suggest that such tokenistic approaches are more likely to reinforce racism and white pupils' feelings of 'differentness', even superiority (Troyna, 1987). However, the 'three Ss' approach has proved to be remarkably resilient and, as a corollary, antiracist education continues to be seen as threatening, divisive, politically contentious and, above all, inappropriate to primary education (see Carrington and Troyna, 1988).

The evidence suggests, then, that there are professional and political objections to the infusion of antiracism into science teaching and primary education. But teachers are agents of change, and if antiracism is to secure a firm toe-hold in the way primary science teaching is organised and administered, we will need to develop ways through which anxieties are assuaged and barriers to change are overcome. Now, as we have already hinted, in the context of diminishing power and responsibility for change at the local level, we may have to look to the centre for the source of legitimation of antiracism. Following from this, we need to establish the extent to which centrally prescribed policies and guidance might expedite changes in primary science along antiracist lines.

Centralisation and its priorities

A clue to these could be found in the publication of two government documents in 1985. The first of these documents was *Education for All*, the final report of a committee set up in 1979 and chaired in its late stages by Lord Swann. This was charged to look at the education of children of ethnic minority origin. In the same month that *Education For All* was published, *Science 5–16: A Statement of Policy* appeared as part of the DES 'Curriculum Matters' series. The publications were similar in so far as both reaffirmed a commitment to equality of opportunity. For the Swann report, as it was generally known, this commitment was expressed through the organising principle of 'education for all'. It demanded of central government the need to recognise cultural pluralism and the practices to which it gives rise as 'a priority area for curriculum development' (DES, 1985a, p.361). Similarly, *Science 5–16* addressed the principle of equality of opportunity through the theme of 'science for all' in which it asserted the need for 'genuinely equal curricular opportunities' for boys and girls (DES, 1985b, p.5). But here the similarities ended. Whilst the Swann committee had called for changes in the organisation and delivery of education to accommodate ethnic and cultural diversity, *Science 5–16* advocated an assimilationist stance in which pupils studying science were encouraged to develop 'an appreciation of a significant part of our cultural heritage' (DES, 1985b, p.3). Simply put, *Science 5–16* promoted a vision of society characterised by consensus, unity, cohesion and, above all, homogeneity within which the curriculum should take on a pivotal role. Along with contemporary DES documents such as *Better Schools* (DES, 1985c), *Science 5–16* embraced a conception of society in which the illusory belief in social cohesion prevailed over the reality of disharmony, conflict and dissension in British society. In sharp contrast, and despite its many weaknesses, *Education for All* did, at least, recognise how the divisive nature of contemporary Britain might be exacerbated by the perpetuation and legitimation of a racist education system.

On this view, the committee implored central government to initiate changes which recognised the legitimacy of cultural pluralism and the debilitating influence of racism. But, of course, for central government to have acknowledged the legitimacy of this interpretation it would have needed also to come to terms with the divisive effects of other aspects of its political and economic programme.

Such a prospect could not be entertained. Needless to say, then, the fortunes of these documents have differed greatly. *Education for All* has been consigned to the annals of history and its impact on educational policymaking at the DES has been minimal. *Science 5–16*, on the other hand, uniquely in the 'Curriculum Matters' series, was assigned the status of a policy statement, and later formed the basis of the National Curriculum Science Working Group's thinking.

If the messages inferred from the reception and influence of these documents are that central government is reluctant to sanction antiracist perspectives in primary science (or anywhere else, for that matter), the Education Reform Act and initiatives which stem from it confirm this. Of particular interest here is the interim report of the Science Working Group (SWG). Central to this report, it would seem, is the same concept, 'science for all'. Thus:

The science education we want to promote should be accessible to all pupils. It should be broad enough to cover the economic, social, personal and ethical implications of science, balanced enough to reflect the inter-relatedness of physics, chemistry and biology; relevant to pupils' everyday experience and to today's world; and sufficiently differentiated to be equally accessible to different ability groups, to girls as well as boys, and to pupils of all social, cultural and ethnic backgrounds.
(DES, 1987, pp 11–12).

Implicit in this version of 'science for all' are two distinctive prescriptions. First, there is the quantitative interpretation of 'science for all'; namely, a commitment to maximising access to science education. For this it finds enthusiastic support from Brenda Prestt. Writing in *Education in Science* six months after the publication of the report, Prestt asserts that 'the setting of attainment targets' represents the move 'which will, at last, ensure that all children of primary school age will receive the early science education which is their entitlement' (Prestt, 1988, p.11). Now, we might agree that the National Curriculum could obviate some of the more blatant forms of discrimination which, amongst other things, have resulted in the under-representation of female students in science subjects. However, the promise of an entitlement curriculum which is implied by the phrase 'science for all' can only be realised if the report also prompts fundamental *qualitative* changes to science education. In other words, generating opportunities to follow a science curriculum which retains racist and sexist impulses is not a commendable reform. If 'science for all' is to presage such changes it needs to imply more than a commitment to numbers.

This brings us to the second feature of the SWG's definition. The assertion that science education needs to be 'sufficiently differentiated to be equally accessible' to a range of ethnic, cultural and gender groups does, on the face of it, imply that important qualitative changes to science education *will* emanate from the report. But we have reservations about this, for two reasons. First, as Richard Hatcher (1987) and others have pointed out, contemporary educational policies routinely acknowledge ethnic and cultural diversity in general statements of aims. But in the more detailed and operational curriculum objectives which follow, multicultural education tends to get lost. Hatcher maintains that the incorporation of multicultural objectives in policy documents is largely perfunctory, and it is difficult to dissent from his view. Where, for instance, do these objectives feature in subsequent sections of the SWG report? But, even if they did, we do not consider the broadly sketched outline of multicultural objectives to be compatible with our conception of antiracist education. The notion of 'differentiation', for example, implies sanctioning differences along ethnic lines, highlighting and *institutionalising* them in the organisation and delivery of education. This process has been characterised as 'ethnicist' by Chris Mullard; that is, the 'cultural representation of the ideological form of racism'. For Mullard, ethnicism constitutes

> a set or representations of *ethnic* differences, peculiarities, cultural biographies, histories and practices, which are used to justify specific courses of action that possess the effect of institutionalising ethnic/cultural differences
> (Mullard, 1986, p.11, original emphasis)

Along with Mullard we conceive of these ethnicist policies and practices as anathema to the concept of antiracist education which is intended to encourage alliances between black and white pupils rather than generate divisiveness.

Finding 'space' for anti-racist education

We have responded critically, then, to the SWG's initial conception of 'science for all'; and even in its final report (DES, 1988a), despite a more elaborate enunciation of the principles of equal opportunities and cultural pluralism, we believe that the changes are of degree rather than of kind. Ethnicism continues to prevail as an organising theme of the SWG's interpretation of 'science for all'. Nevertheless, we believe that the vagueness of their statement of intent provides the space for exploration and development. The implementation of a science curriculum which legitimates, in broad terms, an exploration of the economic, social, personal and ethical implications of science education offers an opportunity to explore those issues which might facilitate antiracist understanding of the way society is organised and functions.

From what we have argued so far it should be clear that we see antiracism as comprising more than just changes to the formal curriculum and teaching aids. Of course, changes along these lines are important, and the removal of racist and sexist exemplars in science might go some way towards expediting 'science for all'. But if one of the main aims of antiracist education is 'to challenge the practices and history which support racial injustices and unequal power' (Troyna, 1987) we need to move beyond simply tinkering with curriculum content. As Jeffs reminded us earlier in this chapter, we need to attend to the organisational structure and norms of the school to ensure that these enshrine and promote antiracist principles. They are likely not to if we accept the view that schools are, on the whole, 'profoundly un-democratic institutions' (Jeffs, 1988, p.47).

Our argument, then, is quite simple: to encourage changes in curriculum content whilst leaving intact other aspects of pupils' educational experiences is both futile and, potentially, counterproductive. The case for an inclusive package of reforms has been argued succinctly by Patricia White (1983):

> Guidelines for teaching and the organisational structure of the school are equally necessary, not least since the child acquires a considerable amount of her political knowledge in an informal way through her membership of the educational institution. It would be foolish to have carefully worked out content guidelines whilst leaving teaching procedures and particularly the structure of the school unregulated. (pp. 24–5)

It seems to us that the most logical outcome of this analysis is for the development of community education. Of course, this is a diffuse concept of educational reform which has failed to crystallize into a coherent or uniform entity. At the very least, however, it must deal directly with traditional and entrenched demarcation boundaries in which 'the division between the weak and the powerful is clearly drawn' (Jackson, 1968, p.10). What should be promoted are more democratised relationships between teachers, parents and pupils. This would not only precipitate significant curricular, organisational and pedagogic changes for the school but would also firmly locate the school in the activities and struggles of the local communities. Nor does the current political context necessarily inhibit genuine forms of community education. Indeed, if we accept the arguments of Steve Baron, the current educational agenda provides more ground for a genuine community education than did 'the arid statism and professionalism of social democracy' (Baron, 1988, p.100). Some of the initiatives identified in John Rennie's description of community primary schools in the UK provide clues to ways in which this development could be (and has been) structured along antiracist and antisexist lines (Rennie, 1985).

Antiracist education in primary school

But if community education constitutes the ideal institutional context for antiracist teaching, what specific intra-school strategies does this perspective imply? It follows logically from endorsing the democratisation of relationships that didacticism, the emphasis on teacher exposition and 'the benign authoritarianism,' which underpins it (Ross, 1984) must be eschewed. A more conducive environment would encompass an emphasis on collaborative learning within a non-competitive arrangement. In practice this would mean activating learning through group work (rather than grouping), negotiation between pupils and teachers and, crucially, the involvement of parents in decision-making processes. The exclusion of parents and pupils from involvement in the elucidation and implementation of antiracist principles is not only anathema to those principles but also likely to stir up the forms of resentment witnessed recently in schools and LEAs in the UK.

Although we have drawn attention to particular organisational and pedagogical implications of antiracist approaches we do not see these as the whole story. If antiracism comprised no more or less than a more coherent move towards collaborative learning in which parents are encouraged to play an active role then, with some justification, a number of teachers might argue that they are already engaged in antiracist practices. Antiracism, however, also involves a critical appraisal of what is taught and learnt in the classroom. Multiculturalists have, of course, tended to engage with this matter by advocating the infusion of conventional science teaching with information about what other cultures have contributed to current western scientific knowledge and understanding. This rationalist approach is based on the view that such insights are likely to encourage a greater appreciation of the value and contribution of minority cultures, and in consequence mitigate feelings of cultural superiority. As we have indicated, this conception of change is hinted at through the SWG's espousal of 'science for all'. It is a recommendation we reject entirely. Not only does it degenerate into ethnicist forms of education but its *raison d'etre* appears to be 'make other cultures ('them') more palatable and acceptable to white British pupils ('us')'. The definitive argument against this classic feature of multiculturalist thinking was made in the early 1980s by the Institute of Race Relations (1982) in its submission to the Rampton Committee:

> Just to learn about other people's cultures is not to learn about the racism of one's own. To learn about the racism of one's own culture, on the other hand, is to approach other cultures objectively' (p. iv)

From this perspective, attention is focused on 'us' not 'them' and the concern becomes: to encourage pupils to take a critical stance towards the way society is organised, the values on which it is based, the ways in which power is exercised and by whom. It also insists that we need to question an educational system in which certain understandings and interpretations are routinely excluded from classrooms in western democratic societies. Such an enterprise is geared towards much more than the individual conversion of pupils; it is a project directed towards encouraging pupils to explore the way in which racism rationalises and helps perpetuate injustice and the differential power accorded to groups in society. This, then, is the priority.

Of course, our proposals could be construed as compatible with those principles enunciated in contemporary policy documents on science teaching and primary education. This may come as a surprise to those readers whose concept of antiracist education owes more to the *Daily Mail* and the *Sun* than to the authentic antiracist approaches operating in a range of schools and applauded by HMI in some of its recent inspections (DES, 1988b).

When confronted with a statement of the principles underlying antiracist education, teachers of science (which now means all primary school teachers) may well reflect on the striking similarity between antiracist educational principles and many of the standard procedures of science teaching.

Carrington and Troyna (1988) have suggested a number of principles which are fundamental to antiracist education, they include:

1 The adoption of a non-didactic approach to learning, and the rejection of the 'teacher legitimated knowledge' model (the Mastermind Syndrome), with its inherent value-laden and potentially controlling stance.
2 Value being placed upon cooperation and collaboration in learning.
3 The importance of negotiation in the learning process.
4 The evolution of a 'partnership in learning' between teacher and pupils.
5 The acceptance of a range of differing and possibly conflicting points of view.
6 The acceptance of rational and independent argument.

Such principles would be instantly recognisable to any teacher familiar with the work of Bruner or Stenhouse, and to those who recognise the importance of learning rather than 'being taught', and who acknowledge that the process of learning may be more valuable than the product. As Townsend also pointed out in Chapter 4, there is here a great deal in common with the goals of primary science learning.

These antiracist educational principles, in another form, translate directly into guidelines for effective science teaching in the primary classroom. We need look no further than the SWG interim report for confirmation of the intent (DES, 1987):

> Children do not acquire knowledge and understanding, skills and attitudes through a narrowly prescribed programme in which they are told or trained. Understanding and competence comes through the children's active engagement with learning experiences . . . (Section 52)

> [Science Education] . . . should help to develop . . . attitudes such as willingness to tolerate uncertainty, to co-operate with others, to give honest reports and to think critically (Section 37)

> There is an important role for the teacher as enabler in the process: the teacher may interact with the pupil, raise questions, build in appropriate challenges and offer new ways of thinking (Section 40)

These are not isolated quotations, but are symptomatic of the tenor of the whole document. Science is to be learned in schools in a non-didactic and investigative way. Children are to be encouraged to raise questions, to be co-operative, to respect the opinions of others, to tolerate uncertainty, and to 'reflect critically'. At a philosophical level, very few teachers would disagree with the aspirations expressed in the SWG interim report, and at a practical level, many teachers employ such principles as a matter of course in their own pursuit of effective science education. Given then, that so many of the principles by which science is most effectively learned in primary schools are also those of antiracist education, surely primary science has no excuse for not being in the vanguard of multicultural/antiracist practice? The very methodology by which we, as teachers, encourage the learning of science, is also the best vehicle for antiracist education, and although there may be reasons for turning away from the commitment and responsibility that this brings, there certainly can be no excuses for doing so.

However, antiracism does not begin and end with process-models of change; nor is it limited only to changes in the formal curriculum. It is, above all, an holistic programme of educational reform which has implications for all areas of the pupil's educational experience. This may seem radical and uncompromising. However, in the context of increasing racist harassment in primary and secondary schools, at a time when racist views figure prominently in the attitudes and beliefs of 'the Thatcher generation' of youngsters (Williams, 1986) and the conservative restoration of educational ideas is being realised through the Education Reform Act, we believe that the principles of antiracism we have alluded to are both timely and pertinent. What do you think?

Chapter 8

Questions of Policy: Some Lost Opportunities in the Making of Primary Science

Mike Watts

Introduction

It is always easy to criticise policy. Science education has changed considerably in the last few years and is still changing. Much of this change has been as a result of policies made at different levels – not just at national level, but at authority and school level too. And, in my view, change has been for the better: for example, we are moving slowly to a stage of much more scientific literacy for many more people. There have been some lapses, and the active promotion of multicultural and antiracist science is one of them. Policy in science education has been sharply and roundly criticised on these grounds, for instance, by Gill and Levidow (1987) amongst many others.

The links between policy and practice are always tenuous, and the two are not always as well connected as, perhaps, they should be. In the context of multicultural and antiracist education, critics have berated the same policies for being unworkable, for being implemented over-zealously, lacking direction, being too restrictive and so on. In this chapter I take a particular line which has been an abiding source of concern and worry, in different forms, over many years. My interest lies in exploring the relationship of the individual to the mainstream: the tension between personal knowledge and 'public knowledge'. For instance, I would want to ask questions like: How does a child of Indian or West Indian (or any other cultural) background begin to connect with the bulk of school science? What do science education policies have to say about helping such children come to terms with science? Can teachers begin to challenge their own prejudices and bias through their teaching of science? What actually happens in school classrooms? These may not be the first questions on everyone's lips, but wait awhile.

Science can be seen very much as a culture in itself: C.P. Snow wrote in that vein in the early sixties. The 'culture' of science can be a world of its own and not everybody has (or, perhaps, wants) access to it. Some people (my neighbours, for example) express open pride that they were 'no good' at science (or maths) at school – and there's no quicker way to clear a space in a crowded party than to respond to 'And what do you do?' with 'I teach physics'.

As Snow (1959) says:

> A good many times I have been present at gatherings of people who, by the standards of traditional culture, are thought highly educated and who have with considerable gusto been expressing their incredulity at the illiteracy of scientists. Once or twice I have been provoked and have asked the company how many of them could describe the second law of thermodynamics. The response was cold: it was also negative.

We know some answers to some parts of my first question. There has been considerable research into the kind of sense children make of concepts in science. The *Learning in Science* Project (Osborne, 1983), for instance, has logged a great deal of important work, and has been enhanced by other research outcomes (see for example, Driver *et al.*, 1985; Osborne and Freyberg, 1985; SPACE project, 1990). But all of this research has looked at the clash of cultures (or of 'two worlds', as Joan Solomon (1983) calls it) between scientific knowledge and 'everyday knowledge'; between commonsense and science. There has been nothing much to help answer questions about the relationships between particular cultures and science, or how science education can help challenge racism.

Government policy

What do successive policy statements say about multicultural science education? At first glance, not a lot. More recently there are some references but you have to look hard and interpret carefully. As was pointed out in the previous chapter, science was the first part of the school curriculum to be graced with a Policy Statement from the Department of Education and Science (DES, 1985b) – probably because science is seen to be such an important aspect of school life. As curriculum matters change so rapidly, that document now seems dated. It still, however, represents a significant statement about school science and is worth examining in some detail. For example, paragraph 9 suggests that science education can promote a view of science as a cultural activity. It should:

encourage . . . an appreciation of (science as) a significant part of our cultural heritage and an insight into man's place in the world which will complement the contribution of other elements in the school curriculum.

Paragraph 12 urges a continuous review of the content of science education:

in the light of changes and developments in science and technology in the wider world.

In paragraph 26 it goes on to say that the content of science education, particularly in the case of primary science, should be such that it can:

(a) wherever possible be related to the experiences of the children;
(b) in accordance with their stages of development, provide them with knowledge and understanding of scientific ideas to help them understand their own physical and biological environments and to understand themselves;
(c) where possible, lay foundations for a progressively deepening knowledge and understanding of scientific concepts and facts that will be useful to them as citizens;
(d) include examples of the applications of science to the real-life problems, including those of technology.

More recently and more specifically, the Science Working Group's final report summarised their view on 'Science and Cultural Diversity' (DES, 1988a) by stressing that:

• in designing learning activities and assessment tasks, care should be taken to avoid ethnic and/or cultural bias;
• pupils own experiences in relation to diet, nutrition, energy, health, the ecosystem and cultural diversity should be used as a basis for learning, so that they can genuinely be agents of that learning;
• the teacher does not adopt a narrow view of 'correctness' – for example, in a discussion about diet or alternative technologies.

Unfortunately, some of this emphasis is lost in the National Curriculum 'Document' for Science (DES, 1989c), but more of that later. So what, then, is the problem? My question now becomes: How would it feel to be a child doing science at school, who is Indian, West Indian or any other minority group? Would the science being taught be relevant to my experiences? allow me greater understanding of myself? enhance my self image? Put another way, does school science positively encourage the customs, lifestyles, traditions and scientific achievements of people in *my* culture to be represented in a way that helps to explain the value, meaning and role of the customs in their lives?

Wait a minute, I hear you say. Those are nonsense questions. After all, science is science. It may have a culture of its own but that culture is based on facts and figures, laws and principles, theories and universal constants – it has nothing to do with world cultures, individuals or society. Has it?

Deciding on science and school science

In a general sense, everyone knows what science is. For example, it is

(a)   about hypotheses and 'fair tests';
(b)   what scientists do in laboratories;
(c)   not art or sociology.

Of course we know in a more specific sense that it is a lot more than that. We seldom ask 'Who decides what science is?' because it seems like one of those child-like questions 'Who first invented music?' or 'Who gave the trees their names?'. There is a real sense in which people *do* decide what science is. The government, for example, provides research funds through two different bodies – the Science and Engineering Research Council (SERC) and the Economic and Social Research Concil (ESRC). If an organisation is planning research into AIDS, for instance, someone must decide if they are doing scientific research or social research. In the case of AIDS it could be either or both. There is a considerable literature about what is science, what isn't and who decides, and the interested reader might start with some excellent books like Barnes and Edge (1982) or Albury and Schwartz (1982).

Clearly, this line of discussion is based on the idea that it is people who actually decide what is science, rather than it being decided by science itself. There are those who think that 'nature leads us where it will' and that science has a kind of natural progress without any reference to humankind. It is convenient to hand over responsibility to 'nature', but most recent sociologists of science are, quite reasonably, willing to return the responsibility to scientists and policymakers. They can't duck the issue – it is *they* who decide.

The common image of science is that it is an impersonal, objective quest for factual descriptions of physical reality, whatever that means. Within this picture, the world exists in an absolute sense such that true discoveries can be made by suitably trained observers (scientists). That is, the discovery of fundamental laws of nature, principles or universal constants does not depend on *who* does the observing or discovering, or which country, culture or social group they belong to. In other words, science is said to be a-personal and a-cultural. Science, say some, is an expression of the patterns and regulations of nature, regardless of geography, social or personal disposition. And within this image, physics is often seen as the most pure in form, the hardest of the 'hard' sciences. From this position, all other sciences are seen to be more 'soft' or 'human' (as in the expression the 'human sciences'). Schrödinger, the Nobel physicist, said:

> From all physical research the subjective intrusion of the researcher is rigorously barred so that the purely objective truth about inanimate nature may be arrived at. Once this truth is finally stated it can be put to the test of experiment by anybody and everybody all the world over, and always with the same result. Thus far physics is entirely independent of the human temperament and this is put forward as its chief claim to acceptance. (Schrödinger, 1966)

In recent years this image of science – and of physics – has shifted a little, particularly in the writings of philosophers and sociologists of science like Toulmin (1961), Lakatos (1970) and particularly Kuhn (1962). The shift is still an issue of some debate and many scientists, and their sponsors, still operate within the traditional view – not least because they fail (or are unwilling) to see how philosophical arguments can affect their daily activities. Arguably, perhaps, no one scientist would stick to this picture of science completely and all of the time. However, as Stenhouse (1985) points out, science at a superficial and popular level is often thought to be constituted by 'facts', by 'objective reality', by what can be observed and measured, even 'in the minds of some people who should know better'.

It is not my intention to delve too deeply into the debate on the nature of scientific knowledge. My purpose is to explore some of its implications for science in schools. It is possible, though, to ask some questions about how scientists select what they are going to explore. Presumably they choose to find some answers to the pressing problems of the time, like acid rain, the 'greenhouse effect', damage to the ozone layer or the search for gravitons. These in turn are only pressing because they come from within a particular 'cultural milieu'. My questions are not so much about whether ozone or gravity, for instance, are universal entities or whether world scientists agree that they are, but whether scientists from differing cultural traditions would even consider gravity and the search for gravitons a research domain worth probing at all. As Schrödinger (1966) goes on to say:

> the engaging of one's interest in a certain subject and in certain directions must necessarily be influenced by the environment, or what may be called the cultural milieu or the spirit of the age in which one lives. In all branches of our civilisation there is one general world outlook dominant and there are numerous lines of activity which are attractive because they are the fashion of the age, whether in politics or in art or in science. These also make themselves felt in the 'exact' science of physics.

At the moment, the world outlook that is currently dominant in science is that of Western European and North American cultures. 'World' science at the moment is white, male, middle-class, Western European science, and it is this science which governs what scientists do, what problems they try to tackle, and what research they get funding for. And this in turn influences the kind of science taught in schools.

So who decides what *school* science is to be? Until very recently school science has been dictated by a wide range of individuals and groups – universities, textbook writers, curriculum development projects, schools, examination boards, classroom teachers, science advisers, school governors and so on. Nowadays, it is the Secretaries of State for Education at the Department of Education and Science who decide – through the Education Reform Act and the workings of the National Curriculum.

What is science for all?

So what of all of this so far? Well, we can say that science is shaped by culture and society, and that school science is most clearly defined and decided by a subset of the same culture and society. The obvious observation then must be that it can come as no surprise that science in schools reflects the dominant culture from the dominant society. Obviously, science in schools will be Western, white, male, middle-class science. And that is the way it is: there's a sense in which it cannot but help reflect the values of the dominant culture. But should it stay that way? If school science is defined by society, cannot it be redefined to reflect a multicultural society?

School science has to serve many functions and some of these arise from the general aims and ambitions we have for science in schools. Some aims for multiculturalism have usually been given expression through policies for science education at governmental levels and below, for example through the policy of the Association for Science Education (ASE, 1981) or Secondary Science Curriculum Review (1983). The history of science education indicates that it has always been the domain of the elite (Layton, 1984), and latterly a selected elite – the 'most able' (however defined). It is only very recently that curriculum development has moved towards broad and balanced 'science for all'. A major aim of multicultural education might be to promote mutual respect and understanding between people of different cultures, leading to harmonious and peaceful co-existence. And as the Association for Science Education (1986) say

> Science remains a vital and integral part of this education and cannot escape its share of responsibility and effort in achieving this aim.

Three more specific aims for science education come from the work of the Secondary Science Curriculum Review (1983) and give a particular framework for multicultural science education. These are that, throughout school science, students should have opportunities to:

- study those aspects of science that are essential to an understanding of oneself and of one's personal well-being;
- gain some understanding of the historical development and contemporary cultural significance of scientific principles and theories;
- appreciate that past scientific explanations were valid in their time and that early technologies are still valid in some cultural contexts.

Although the aims of the SSCR have been largely secondary orientated, they have been careful to ensure they are appropriate to all children studying science. Moreover, they were accepted by the DES as the background to their initial policy statement, and some flavour of this remains in Attainment Target 17 (the Nature of Science) in the National Curriculum.

How, then, should we interpret current policy? For instance, to whom does 'our' refer in the expression 'our cultural heritage'? Is 'our' culture the same as the nation's culture, or is it to do with pupils' own experiences? And is 'our' culture somehow synonymous with 'man's' so that they both refer to the same thing?

These are difficult questions, not just for the authors of policy statements but also for any writers of textbooks and curriculum materials about science. The problem concerns that predominant image of science as a-personal and a-cultural, or culture-neutral. The suggestion is that our nation's science is the same all over the world – British science is the same as Western European science is the same as 'world' science. It underplays the tension between some kind of international or universal science (which is exactly the same and equally relevant to everyone) and culturally determined science (which has relevance only to some cultures in response to their needs and circumstances).

That is, science is seen as being capable of smoothing out all the differences. Unlike philosophy or art, say, where cultural influence is an essential ingredient (whether German, Spanish, French, African, Greek, Italian), science authors, writers, or funding bodies do not admit to different influences. There is little or no recognition of cultural diversity, of either the contributions made by differing cultures or of the diverging routes, assumptions and expectations of other sciences.

So what do policy statements mean by the 'wider world'? It would be nice to think that the reviews of content they have in mind would take in a discussion of oriental medicine, Japanese agriculture or African technology. Unfortunately, if we look at the content areas of the National Curriculum, there are few such indications.

The National Curriculum

In an important paragraph of the report of the National Curriculum Working Party for Science, the authors state they begin from a child centred perspective. The child, they say, is the agent of his or her own learning in science. Children's learning in science is linked by analogy to the way that scientists put forward ideas, hypotheses and principles when faced with new phenomena.

> Learning in science proceeds in much the same way. A child brings ideas of his or her own to the classroom or laboratory, and the aim of science education is then to adapt or modify these original ideas so as to give them more explanatory power. Viewed from this perspective, it is important that we should take a child's initial ideas seriously so as to ensure that what emerges from them, and the evidence on which it is based, make sense to the child, and are 'his own' or 'her own' (National Curriculum Science Working Group, 1988)

Youngsters' prior knowledge and initial theorising are therefore important as part of the process of reaching a scientific understanding of the
world around them. At any point, the authors say, the 'correct' idea is the
one that is helpful to the learner as far as can be judged from the evidence
available. Ideas change and adapt to find a better fit as new evidence
becomes available, in ways described in more detail by John Meadows in
Chapter 6.

This philosophy of the 'child-as-scientist' is not new but is refreshing
in a policy statement. And of course the analogy of person-as-scientist is
not exclusive to children. It can be useful to describe people's explanations and ways of imagining which are 'adjacent' to orthodox science;
George Kelly has built an entire philosophical and psychological theory
on that parallel (Kelly, 1955). People have 'spectacles' or 'goggles' (Pope
and Watts, 1988) through which events and phenomena are seen, and
through which they interpret and understand what they see. As much as
we want children to evaluate the personal models as constructed through
their spectacles, we also want teachers to evaluate and re-evaluate theirs.

For example, 'race' itself can be considered a scientific concept. What
if we are considering themes in science to do with 'diversity and classification of living things' or 'variation, inheritance and evolution'? These
are now parts of the statutory primary curriculum (DES, 1989c) and
children are expected to have knowledge and understanding of them. For
example Attainment Target 4 (Genetics) requires that children should

- know that human beings vary from one individual to the next (level
  1);
- be able to measure simple differences between each other (level 2);

whilst Attainment Target 2 (The Variety of Life) stipulates that children
should

- be able to sort living things into broad groups according to observable
  features (level 3).

How will the notion of 'racial types' be tackled? Will teachers avoid the
issue, or launch into the 'characteristics or features of various racial
types'? How will they temper their 'goggles' by modifying their own
understandings, their own personal theories? How will they differentiate
with respect to the pupils' cultural background? Barbara Wyvill has
offered one approach in Chapter 1. But as Michael Vance (1987) says:

None of the texts commonly used by schools questions the arbitrary manner in which subdivisions of human groups are made when the text classifies them into 'races'. Why choose hair colour or skin tone? Why not blood groups? In Europe people have differing skin colours, hair types and frequencies of gene for blood group A. Yet somehow Europeans manage to be presented as part of the same race – the white and blonder members being slightly more pure, perhaps.

Back to policy, however. The National Curriculum Science Working Group's aim, they say, is to promote science education as accessible to all pupils (DES, 1988a):

> It should be broad enough to cover the economic, social, personal and ethical implications of science; balanced enough to reflect the interrelatedness of physics, chemistry and biology; relevant to pupils' everyday experience and today's world; and sufficiently differentiated to be equally accessible to different ability groups, to girls as well as boys and to pupils of all social, cultural and ethnic backgrounds.

The knowledge, understanding, skills and attitudes they outline are interlinked with the nature and quality of learning experiences. Knowledge and understanding in science is explored through a series of themes:

- living things and their interaction with the environment,
- materials and their interactions,
- energy and matter,
- forces and their effects,
- earth, atmosphere and space.

Skills include:

- raising scientific questions,
- exploring everyday experiences,
- measuring and using equipment,
- searching for patterns in data,
- investigating and reporting systematically.

Attitudes include:

- curiosity,
- perserverance,
- cooperation with others,
- sensitivity to living things.

The group provide a series of criteria, in the form of questions, which need to be prominent in the selection of appropriate classroom learning experiences. Criteria such as, will the learning experience:

- stimulate curiosity?
- appeal to both girls and boys and to those of all cultural backgrounds?
- offer opportunities to work cooperatively and to communicate scientific ideas to share?

To apply these in such a way as to make multicultural science a reality, what kind of policy is needed?

What kind of policy should there be?

What has been written, one might say, seems fair enough. The Science Working Group are quite clear that they are trying not to be prescriptive about how and what teaching should take place. They stress that their programmes of study do not constitute a syllabus. Their purpose is to:

> map out the ground to be covered in general terms. It is then for schools and teachers to develop appropriate teaching and learning approaches in the light of their own needs, circumstances and opportunities.

This is very clear but it is also a 'get out' clause. They are playing the game of saying that 'science in schools should be what we say it is – and it is for teachers and schools to differentiate it for pupils'. But there is little or no suggestion in the rest of the document as to how this might be done. Let's say a child newly arrived from Bangladesh or Vietnam brings her/his own ideas of science mediated through their own language; interprets phenomena in terms of their own experiences, cultural norms and values; and accumulates personal evidence that supports those ideas. Will teachers really grant these the status and kudos of (nascent) scientific theories and attempt to give them 'greater explanatory power'? How? Will the end result be judged 'correct' or 'incorrect' science? Will the child be judged to have reached the appropriate attainment target at an appropriate level? There is nothing in the statements on content to suggest any help here. And what happens if there are no children from Bangladesh or Vietnam, but an all white (male?) class? Will teachers not then feel they need to differentiate on the basis of culture?

Perhaps there is some comfort in the policy of the National Curriculum Task Group on Assessment and Testing (1987). They quite properly recommend that assessment tasks should be reviewed regularly for evidence of bias, particularly in respect of gender and race.

But that's all. Nothing about how. It would be illuminating to eavesdrop on a primary moderators' meeting where classroom teachers argue that a child's personal, but idiosyncratic, theories have attained all the 'processes of science' attainment targets. And how can we be assured that teachers' classroom assessments over time are reviewed for evidence of racial bias? We must wait and see.

In a previous article (Nott and Watts, 1987) we attempted to put words into the mouths of policy makers. If they had taken the opportunity, what *might* they have said? Rephrased, for example, paragraph 26 of the DES's policy statement might have said that the criteria for choosing content should also include that it must:

(a) introduce alternative scientific theories (both contemporary and historical) in a way that illustrates cultural diversity and not Western superiority;
(b) recognise science as a cultural determinant, and that 'our' cultural heritage owes (and continues to owe) a considerable debt to early science throughout the world;
(c) set facts, concepts, skills and attitudes in human context so that examples have relevance to both minority and majority groups;
(d) take care that no resource material creates offence with clumsy or insulting caricatures.

It seems to me that these kinds of statements give rise to three basic premises. For instance, based on the words of SSCR (1983), this policy would mean that:

(a) a change is needed in the way science is taught;
(b) each individual teacher has a responsibility to consider the nature of that change and its implications for his/her teaching through science;
(c) those with a curriculum responsibility for science are the most appropriate agents for identifying and implementing the change needed.

It is important that changes in science education are not superficial. In Chapter 7, Barry Troyna and Steve Farrow highlight the sentiments of the Rampton Report, namely that multicultural education allows all children to come to terms with other cultures, whilst antiracist education allows us to come to terms with the racism within our own. If there is a will to make education generally – and science education in particular – sensitive to the needs of *all* youngsters then the changes have to be significant for those involved. The policies we have looked at above seem to want to move in the right direction. But they could do so much more to help determine the cultural values implicit in science and help shape and explore the appropriate areas of concern and awareness with children. What would good practice be within science education? Again, based on the SSCR (1983) my policy would include:

1   Developing a policy for the teaching of science in school from a multicultural perspective in a way that will seek to counter the causes of inequality and prejudice.
2   Ensuring that all members of the school are provided with in-service training to aid them in implementing such a policy.
3   Reviewing approaches to language in science and collaborating with language specialists (for example English as a Second Language teachers) to share expertise.
4   Reviewing resources and assesment techniques to examine their underpinning values.

Within the classroom good practice might include:

1   Adopting a view that sees cultural diversity as a positive advantage, so that use can be made of the varied experiences of youngsters from different cultural backgrounds (as in Chris Hannon's work in Chapter 2).
2   Using all opportunities to challenge stereotyping, prejudice and racism (as in Barbara Wyvill's examples, in Chapter 1).
3   Viewing science and technology as a response to human needs and demonstrating the validity of technology in relation to specific cultural contexts (as illustrated by Mwangi Githui in Chapter 10).
4   Illustrating that science has different implications for individuals in different parts of the world (see Tony Russell's examples from Botswana, in Chapter 9).
5   Setting western science in a historical context which illustrates that it is relatively young in terms of the history of science.

Multicultural education is not just about altering the flavour of the curriculum but is a way of teaching that requires both teachers and learners to challenge their own personal ideas, values, beliefs and attitudes. This approach should permeate everything we do and not just the occasions when there is something 'cultural' on the timetable for the day. And that means a major thrust to achieve genuine multicultural and antiracist education through the medium of science.

Chapter 9

Primary Science and the Clash of Cultures in a Developing Country

Tony Russell

Introduction

It would be very reassuring to know that the content and methods of primary science education were perfectly matched to the needs of children involved. Yet the more one reads and thinks about the complexities of such matching, the more ignorant one feels. One's reaction is to become 'paralysed' into inaction, as a means of avoiding mis-match. Primary teachers without a science background, still the majority here in the UK as elsewhere, feel drawn towards that escape route, and no amount of well-meant exhortation is sufficient to encourage them. The naive hopes and certainties of curriculum planners and developers have so often been wrecked on the rocks of inertia and ignorance which still obstruct the way, towards a curriculum which not only meets the numerous demands made upon it but is also within the professional expertise and confidence of teachers. This is true both for us in Britain today and for countries struggling to become truly independent.

The perception of science by any particular society, the values and beliefs with or against which science must work, the pre-conceptions, mis-conceptions and alternative frameworks which occupy the minds of the population, including children when first entering school, are some of the features of a culture which interact with the content, methods and attitudes of primary science. What has emerged in numerous studies throughout the world, as Mike Watts suggested in Chapter 8, is that science is not as culture-free as has sometimes been thought. Nor do we really understand which beliefs and behaviours characteristic of a particular culture interfere with scientific understanding. It would be arrogant of us, as a former imperial power, to feel that such unanswered questions and practical problems are peculiar to the 'underdeveloped', the 'developing', the 'newly- independent'. I came to the conclusion when working in Botswana that, regardless of the details of the particular national context, the fundamental teaching and learning situations were identical. That must mean that we, in the so-called 'developed' part of the world community, as well as they, can learn through sharing our difficulties and successes, our common experiences and those peculiar to our society.

This chapter therefore raises and addresses some of the questions about science, schooling and the implications for teaching which are common to our own multicultural society and other multicultural societies in the developing world.

The role of science in schooling

Societies throughout history in all parts of the world have concerned themselves with the initiation of the young into adult society. In the Western societies this process has been increasingly transferred from the general context of family and tribe, with religious practices and beliefs bound up in it, to specific contexts called schools, colleges and universities. This shift has tended over a long period to separate the two areas of experience, and to invest the learning in the institutions with a higher value, a greater significance. Indeed, taken to its extreme, this view has led to the conclusion that no learning, or none of any significance, takes place before children are 'schooled'. This absurd idea has, to some extent, stuck around longer in connection with science than, say, language or number. Science still has a hard image. Perhaps in Britain at present the image is hardening, as it is more and more linked with terms like 'high-tech'. Such language intimidates people, especially those whose school experience of science was brief, alienating, and none too happy. Many primary teachers would put themselves in that group.

Yet wherever you look in the world, science is there near the top of any government's list of curriculum subjects. In 1971 the UN produced the World Plan of Action for the Application of Science and Technology to Development. One of its premises was that 'the scientific approach offers the best hope for assisting the developing nations to speed up the process of their all round development'. The National Curriculum puts science on a par with language and maths. This is a typical situation. In Botswana, an ex-British Protectorate, primary pupils face a science paper in the Primary School Leaving Examination. This examination has been, and to some extent remains, the key to secondary education. The science paper was an innovation in 1980. Such changes only come about for political reasons: that is as true here as in Botswana.   Curriculum changes reflect political intentions, sometimes matching pupils' needs and interests, but sometimes not. The tension between these is the inherent dilemma in all institutionalised education: the twin objectives of personal and/or societal benefits. At times one seems to predominate and then a shift occurs, not brought about by pupils or teachers, but by those responsible for steering the course taken by the country – the government of the day.

The economic emphasis of science and central control

Countries which have only relatively recently taken control of their own schools are generally unable to avoid putting stress on the societal objective of education. Nation building predominates, rather than the apparent luxury of personal development and fulfilment. This is very obvious in science education. The typical line of reasoning links national development and prosperity with growth in the 'modern sectors' of the economy (UNESCO, 1980). This in turn creates the need for skilled manpower, technicians, professionals of all kinds, particularly with a science and/or technology base. The assumption is then made that the earlier such 'school subjects' appear on the curriculum, the greater the chance of success in developing economy and bringing the benefits of modern life to the whole population.

The intention is twofold. An elite group of scientists, technicians and professionals applying their science based skills will play their vital part in raising the country from poverty and dependence to wealth and independence. Meanwhile the whole population is to become 'scientifically literate', informed of the benefits which science and its applications in medicine, agriculture, transport, communications, etc. can bring. With such citizens a country would feel greater security for its future development.

Few voices have been raised against this very appealing scenario. Baez (1976) quotes a World Bank economist, Dr Ul Haq, who 'rejects the theory that the stimulation of high growth rates results in the trickling down of wealth to the masses . . . production will go to the well-to-do and not the poor'. Bacchus (1981) agrees that the assumptions of the 1950s and 60s have proved false – the modern sector has not led economic development and its benefits have not trickled down to the poor.

Naturally, primary science has been seen as having a clear part to play in this grand design. It is looked on as the foundation for later teaching and learning. The more centralised the curriculum planning is, the more the actual *content* of the primary syllabus becomes prescribed as the planners attempt to lock it in precisely to the secondary syllabus. The personal interests and needs of particular pupils within their own social contexts are more or less disregarded.

Thus the process of separating the child's two areas of experience is accelerated. The science curriculum grows more and more irrelevant at the same time as the amount of content, the facts so apparently vital to the impending secondary phase, piles up. So any hope of keeping primary science as a valuable part of any child's balanced and rounded education recedes under the pressures of economic necessity, international competitiveness and the planner's desire for neat schemes with clear hierarchies of knowledge and understanding.

To a poor country, forced to participate in the global economy, the centralisation of curriculum planning under the direct control of government thus seems an obvious necessity. Resources are limited, the pressure on the government is to produce particular results in terms of manpower targets, industrialisation, literacy and universal primary education. This pressure comes from within the population itself, as it is exposed to the world more and more through trade, radio, tourism, TV and other disturbers of the traditional views of life. Education, often fashioned on the Western model, helps in this process of raising the expectations of the people. Castle (1972) explains how 'The African wanted the same sort of education his white masters had enjoyed'. Science is right there at the sharp end of all this; the technology of the west is the bright lure which attracts and fascinates the governments and the individual villages alike in so many countries of Africa, Asia and elsewhere.

Externally the pressure is exerted in the same direction, though arising from different causes. Donor countries, like the UK, link their aid to trade in quite blatant ways and so help to keep the now independent countries dependent in a new way. For example, the Overseas Development Administration decided in 1982 that 'It is right at the present time to give greater weight in the allocation of our aid to political, industrial and commercial considerations alongside our basic developmental objective. (O.D.A., 1982)

In education the effect is just as obvious and is really part of the same process. Some call it 'cultural imperialism'. In order to make proper use of the benefits of much western aid, the recipients must have technically skilled personnel to operate and service the machines, etc. Consequently the donors pressurise a country to gear its education system to this process of technological and industrial change. It must be admitted that many recipients appear totally willing to co-operate. Science becomes a key area of study. Experts from the donor countries are financed, scholarships are made available for the most able to study science subjects abroad, grants for books and equipment to set up science departments in universities, teachers' colleges and secondary schools are given priority. The whole process seems to have an inevitability about it and the burden of its logic falls with particular force on the primary teachers of the world.

The demands on teachers

As a group they are ill-equipped to spear-head this revolution. Their governments often emphasise one or more views of science. Each holds its own terrors for the primary teacher. Most popular has been, and remains, the view of science as a body of knowledge – the 'truth' about the natural world. Such a view is peculiarly attractive to traditionally authoritarian societies. The 'truth' is seen as something fixed, which has authority and can be easily transmitted from teacher to pupil. It allows teachers to retain the traditional and expected role of authority and source of knowledge. Pupils in such societies expect and enjoy such clear teaching. They use a mixture of the traditional and the pragmatic in assessing the classroom performance of their teachers. They know that their 'schooling' is functional – a means to a highly desirable end. Escape from poverty, drudgery and domination by the elemental forces of nature is a possibility for those who succeed in the fiercely competitive 'education race'. For vast numbers of pupils this race begins as soon as they enter school. Failure at the end of primary schooling shuts the doors which are only opened by means of secondary education or more. So, the pupils measure teachers by the 'examination pass rate' yardstick and exams generally want facts to the virtual exclusion of all else at primary level. In practice then, the 'good' science teacher in primary schools is the one who 'spoonfeeds' her class, by filling the board with facts to be laboriously copied and subsequently memorised, for later regurgitation in the memory recall game called Primary School Leaving Exams or their equivalent. The dangers inherent in all this are so clear. 'Science' is reduced to factual information about topics chosen by the Ministry of Education, taught and learned in a completely formal, passive manner by all the members of a peer group throughout an entire country, in order to prepare themselves for the national primary exams.

Unfortunately, countries which have adopted this model for their primary science education are often the ones where the primary teachers cannot 'deliver the goods' as it were. They often had little or no science themselves whilst at school. This is particularly true for the many who did not have any secondary education. What science they did encounter in school was almost certainly taught formally and learned by rote, with little or no understanding. So, they are doubly handicapped as teachers, with only the formal model on which to base their own teaching and with enormous gaps in their knowledge and understanding of the topics on the syllabus.

The language of science

One obvious problem is that of vocabulary in science. So many terms are either peculiar to science, or are used in very particular ways, not in keeping with their common usage. In a language such as Setswana many English words have no equivalent. This is the case with names of objects and concepts. For example, whereas science classifies the animal kingdom into several phyla (insects, molluscs, reptiles, mammals, etc), the traditional system in Botswana employs only two terms, 'Ditshidinyana' – the small creatures and 'Diphologolo' – the large creatures. In standard 2, when children are around 7 years old and have been learning English for only a year, the alien term 'insects' is introduced in the science syllabus, as the first step in the 'proper' classification of the 'Ditshidinyana'. The scientific content is thus inevitably experienced to some extent as an unfamiliar, alien part of life, peculiar to school. Teachers are as much part of the local community as the pupils and share their language's limitations. The limitations, as Chapter 4 also showed, are created by the demand that they all learn to look at and think about their environment in the 'whites' terms, using the 'whites' language. A few countries (e.g. Kenya) have attempted to 'localise' the language of science and have created new words. At least it is a reaction which values their own culture and refuses to subjugate it to any Western one. Some would argue that the international nature of science makes it unnecessary to 'localise'. The language of science is 'nation-less' in their eyes and therefore a neutral factor. A quick look at publishers' lists will show the true state of affairs. Mother-tongue publishing of primary science materials is *very* rare, the reason given being that the print run would be too small to make it economic. So, primary teachers have difficulty expanding the brief information contained in the syllabus or handbook, especially when teaching the early years classes, where the mother tongue is the medium of instruction.

I remember my first visit to a school in Botswana. Sitting in a room where history was being taught, I became aware of noise from a class across the way. Looking out I saw the teacher had her class lined up along the wall and was moving along calling out in a loud voice certain words, which the children were attempting to repeat. Though I couldn't hear their soft responses I knew when they were unsatisfactory, because the teacher would hit children round the head. It turned out that the teacher was a student from our college and we were to observe her teaching. Her method became clear when we entered her room. On the blackboard she had pinned her diagram of a bean seed, before and after germination. It was heavily labelled with terms such as micropyle, testa, radical. These were the vital words she had so laboriously and painfully been drumming in to her young non-English speakers. Some could repeat them. Many could not. What use were they to any of them? The only use lay in the future, when the exam would sort out those with good retention and recall.

Lack of resources

To make the situation worse, the lack of funds often leaves the teachers without the support which books can give. Where curriculum developers make attempts to provide guidance, the syllabus handbooks and guidelines they produce can become merely blueprints for lessons which follow the 'suggestions' slavishly. It is sometimes argued that science done in that way is preferable to none at all. So long as science exams remain largely tests of recall, then the formal methods and rote learning match the situation quite realistically. Certainly the pupils and their parents require massive changes in their perception of primary science, before they would happily allow teachers to move far away from the 'body of knowledge' model they have come to expect. Castle (1972) reports that Nyerere's reforms in Tanzania insisted:

> on a dynamic relationship between the neighbourhood, the children and the teachers, . . . based on the principle of learning through activity related directly to the rural life most of the children are destined to live.

But Bacchus (1981) points out that parents in Tanzania were dubious about attempts to ensure that primary education will become more useful in itself and not simply a means to facilitate entry into the secondary schools.

This being the case, primary teachers need to be very confident indeed to depart from the model which is so strongly built and defended by the system in which they were taught and in which they now teach. Yet curriculum developers have often failed to recognise the key role of the class teacher in reform, whether it involves methods or just content. Without the active consent of the teachers, the plans issued from ministries will remain so much talk; theoretical, well-intentioned, but ineffective. The teachers are not culpable in this. They have so often not been involved in the process of change. The new syllabus is suddenly thrust upon them, without adequate, or even any, in-service preparation. Along with the new content there are often demands for radical changes of teaching method: methods which they have never or rarely seen in practice; methods adapted, or merely transferred uncritically, from another context to their own. The report of a 1980 UNESCO meeting of experts on the incorporation of science and technology in the primary school curriculum summed up their opinion as follows:

> The main channel of improvement in primary school science was through the teachers. Experience of curriculum materials development shows that, however sound in theory such materials are, the resources put into developing them are not well used unless teacher education adequately prepares teachers for using them.

Science as a process

'Science as a process' has become increasingly fashionable over the last 30 years, first in the industrialised countries and then the developing countries, as the process of international conference workshops and seminars spread the new orthodoxy round the world. The 1980 UNESCO meeting outlined the principle clearly in its report:

> Scientific principles and methods are essentially the same throughout the world. Those applications of science which meet the greatest needs of each country will determine the curriculum content and particular examples of the science course, but the basic strategies of science (which are universal) will be employed . . . as essential knowledge changes with time and experience, people must learn how to obtain new knowledge and how to evaluate its quality as a basis for their decision making.

Since the content of science syllabuses was difficult to agree on because of changing needs over time and place, the immutability of the scientific processes was a very attractive alternative. Surely *they* were truly culture-free, a genuine international language of science, one which would remain relevant at all times, everywhere. Baez (1976) supported this with:

it is more important that students acquire the frame of mind associated with discovery and enquiry than it is for them to memorise facts whose value may be transitory.

From the class-teacher's point of view, this shift of emphasis from the facts of science to the methods by which it establishes those facts, has sometimes appeared to be no improvement at all. At least with facts you can list them, memorise them, repeat them. It's all clearly defined and limited, with topics and key facts set out in the syllabus. Teachers and their pupils know that the exams will only attempt to measure their mastery of those facts.

The processes of science, on the other hand, appear to lack clear limits; there is the element of 'open-endedness', the enquiry, the investigation, the search. A syllabus which emphasises the execution of the various processes by the pupils, with suggestions for topics from which teachers and/or pupils make their choices, is more threatening than one which emphasises the 'body of knowledge'. For a teacher who has probably never carried out an investigation in a scientific way, the prospect of organising their class to work in that way is daunting. It has little attraction then, if it is obvious that the science exams set by the Ministry will not attempt to assess the pupils' practical skills, or probably even their knowledge of the processes. In this situation, common in countries where the importation of the 'process-centred' type of curriculum has occurred, the primary teachers remain unable and unconvinced. Harlen (1982) reported that the head of an Indonesian primary development project

> pointed out teachers' inability to use process skills in their teaching and that 90% of questions in the end of Primary exam test only recall. The present system provides no motivation to use process skills.

Why abandon the relative safety of the formal recitation of scientific facts for the potentially chaotic and unpredictable demands of practical work, which is fundamental to a proper understanding of scientific processes? If their own lack of practical experience is not sufficient reason, teachers point to the lack of material resources – the equipment which practical work implies. In quick succession, other very legitimate difficulties are pointed out. Class sizes are often enormous and in some cases teachers are attempting to cope with more than one class at a time, e.g. in India. Even group work is not the simple matter it is sometimes reckoned to be. Can anyone really keep 80 pupils learning in small groups, whilst dutifully 'going the rounds'? And how will colleagues react to the inevitable noise and disturbance? Even the newly qualified young teacher who may have been briefly exposed to the processes of science during training, will need enormous courage, confidence, skill and determination to introduce such revolutionary teaching methods into the traditional school so common all over the world. Many, most even, either don't try or if they do, they soon conform. The old methods, relying on a teacher knowing their subject and being able to relay it to the pupils, are of proven worth. The new, the practical, looks and sounds unlikely to produce the results the Ministry of Education looks for in the exams, so why even attempt it? As ex-colleagues in Botswana and in-service trainees from India and Indonesia have made clear to me, while the syllabus remains so full of topics, how can they adopt the much more time-consuming practical methods? The two demands don't match.

The impact of cultural differences on science learning

In addition to, and perhaps more significant than, all these legitimate reservations, is the cultural one. For pupils to experience the processes of investigation, testing, devising experiments, etc., there has to be a radical shift in the 'sub-culture' which is the primary class. Pupils are not used to being given such freedom, and teachers are not used to being regarded as on a par with their pupils, as 'fellow-investigators'. The cultural norms are offended by the curriculum philosophy. Whereas questioning and discussion are encouraged in primary classrooms and in British society generally, the very idea of young children doing such things in many societies is unacceptable. Durojaiye (1980) comments on this from the African perspective by saying:

> Whilst the school encourages talking, the exchange of ideas, questioning and curiosity, the home may put a premium on being seen but not heard as a hall-mark of good behaviour. The child's school experience often belongs to an entirely different world from his home experience.

In Botswana, for example, even adults traditionally do not ask direct questions, but approach their requests or queries 'obliquely', circling the issue repeatedly. European expatriates like myself had some difficulty in handling this. In class, the students at the teacher training college, or pupils in teaching practice schools, seemed incredibly passive. Requests and encouragement to raise questions, to give their opinions, to discuss – these were not easy for them to respond to. Obviously they were not in the habit of doing such things, certainly not in school. If a culture, or just a family, elevates adults, regardless of their skill or knowledge, to a position of unquestioned superiority in status and authority, then the notion of young children being accorded virtual equal rights with the adults, particularly in the school context, is bound to cause a clash.

This issue is at the philosophical heart of science education and in that sense clashes with culture on the level of beliefs, ideas about the natural world, its phenomena and their meanings. As Castle (1972) put it:

> The developing countries are at the receiving end of a disturbing impact of western technology and alien values, which conflict with their own world view.

Fundamental to the scientific view of the world is the belief that as knowledge increases, through careful and systematic observation and experiment, our views will change. New theories will be put forward, be tried and ultimately discarded, or absorbed into the 'body of knowledge'. Change, growth, new ideas – these are the source of so much of the excitement and attraction which science has for many people. It seems a long way from the narrow popular view, held apparently by some curriculum planners, that science established *the* truth, once and for all. Science actually increases our ignorance and perplexity to some extent, the answering of today's question leading to two or more new ones tomorrow. This element of quest, with its ritual ways of working ('the scientific method'), its beliefs, its laws, its learned ones, its special language, is not so different from other human enterprises. Religion and the arts are not a million miles away from science, though some would attempt to keep them separated.

Can anyone doubt the creativity and imagination involved in the development of scientific concepts? The use of metaphorical language, the construction of 'models' to act as vehicles for mental activity, the imagery drawn from the everyday world of experience, all indicate how much of a fully human activity science is. Ortony (1975) says

> The vivid imagery arising from metaphorical comprehension encourages memorability and generates of necessity a better, more insightful, personal understanding. But also it is a very effective device for moving from the well-known to the less well-known.

So magnets 'attract' or 'repel'; forces 'act'; species 'adapt', and so on. The coldly rational, entirely logical, emotionless scientist exists in popular mythology. In reality, such a person would lack essential human qualities, vital to the progress of scientific explanations of the natural world, as well as to their application in ways which do not threaten that natural order.

In that respect, the beliefs and ideas of a traditional animistic society like that found in many parts of Africa are parallel to those of a modern scientific society. Hawes (1979) makes the point that:

> No valid consideration of the school curriculum can be made without consideration of a child's view of causal relationships and no analysis of causal relationships in African children can be made without consideration of the nature of their spiritual beliefs.

We must see the children's ideas of Chapter 6 in this context.

But Ingle and Turner (1981) warn that traditional culture will not survive untouched.

> The traditional belief system founded on mythology becomes the cement of society and the framework on which day to day events depend. There is an unspoken assumption that the image of science described by the imported curricula is 'correct' and that it is suitable for all pupils. This assumption is reinforced by the view that 'science is science' wherever it is taught.

Thus in the so-called 'non-scientific' culture of many countries the methods and assumptions of science appear to be in obvious collision with cultural practices and beliefs. The introduction at ministerial level of curriculum reform which exacerbates the clash, either through ignorance of the forces at work, or through a shallow quick-fix approach, has done little to extend most primary pupils' experience of genuine scientific enquiry. Both the content, in its language and its organisation, and the methods of science are experienced as being 'from outside' the culture of the majority of primary children and their teachers. A generation or two ago within their societies, vast numbers of illiterate, unschooled adults formed the communities in which today's pupils struggle to make some sort of sense out of their two lives – one in home and community, the other at school.

School science seems to strike at the heart of so many traditional beliefs and customs embedded in the religion, the agriculture, the health, the family life and so much else. Medicine is an example of the conflict between traditional and scientific: 'traditional' medicine has not died out in developing countries, in spite of education and the provision of Western, scientific medicine. My students and colleagues in Botswana happily consulted the traditional doctors, as well as visiting the clinic. For them, 'cultural clash' was dealt with in a very pragmatic way. Their traditional system of beliefs and ideas was not abandoned in favour of the 'truth' as revealed by science. Rather the two 'bodies of knowledge', the two 'ways of working' co-existed in them, with some overlap but with no obvious effort to reconcile points of disagreement. Castle (1972) asks:

> Can we assume that African traditions are being changed in the sense that Africans are giving up old ways for new? In fact, they are grafting new ways on the old.

This view is supported by Smart (1981) who says:

> Many Africans are animists and belong to the traditional religions of the continent. These religions have their own unique ways of perceiving man and nature and the relationships that bind them. The metaphysical world view informs African indigenous education, and this, in turn, affects the attitudes of their adherents to modern education, particularly those parts of it that are empirical and scientific. There is some evidence to show that many educated Africans have multiple explanations for most phenomena; one scientific (which they learnt at school) and the other (to them the 'real' ones) caused by a supernatural manifestation.

Jahoda (1970) summed up his research in Ghana with:

> It is possible to venture at least the tentative conclusion that the younger generation of Ghanaian students have achieved 'a state of cognitive co-existence' between modern ideas and values and some traditional African beliefs.

Learning Outside School

All this reminds us vividly of the fact that pupils do not come to school 'blank' with respect to science or any other school subject, a point made by Driver et al. (1985) in their research in children's science learning in the United Kingdom. Children come with a complex framework of experiences already in place. Incorporated into that framework is a vocabulary which has been acquired and put successfully to use at home and in the community. They have tried out their ideas in practical ways. They have seen their parents, and other older members of their social group, apply their knowledge of the natural world and their skills at solving problems, e.g. locating underground water before digging a well, building a well-insulated house from local natural materials, preserving meat when the hunters bring back more than can be immediately eaten. Through personal experience and pre-school education at home, pupils are already grappling intellectually and practically with the subject matter of science. This has always been so in every place and time throughout human history. If this is true of children growing up and going to school in their own culture, how much more true it must be of children whose home culture is different from the host culture in which school is set, as is the case for many children of Asian origin, for example, in Britain.

Yet our European arrogance lets us think that before Western scientific ideas were introduced into Africa, Asia and elsewhere, there was an enormous 'blank space' in the knowledge and skills of their people. We choose to overlook, or fail to even notice, the indigenous ideas and skills which have successfully sustained societies in a variety of locations around the world. Many examples of applied science and technology originated in Africa, such as soap making and salt extraction.

So we fool ourselves if we think we begin science when children start school. We also fool ourselves if we think we can ignore what knowledge and skills children already have. We don't, for example, know enough yet about cognitive development in detail, to be clear about the mechanisms by which these cultural, as opposed to school, elements of experience make their contribution to that development. The call for such knowledge has been largely ignored over a long period. Otaala (1981) wrote

> If we have to build the necessary linkage of studies of the learning process and curriculum development, we will need to know much more about the African child than we do to date.

This was seven years after a UNESCO seminar proposed an International Centre for the Study of Concept Development in African Children.

Matching children and teaching

Such ignorance at the fundamental level admitted by Professor Otaala should be openly acknowledged by all of us engaged in primary science education, and we could usefully begin by exploring the conceptual learning of children from all cultures in our society.

The rote-learning of children in Africa is essentially the same as that going on in any British classroom, where often, and particularly in science, the cognitive level of the child and the concept have been mismatched (DES, 1978). For the children, the outcome is the same; so much of what is learned remains 'school-knowledge', unrelated and un-applied in the wider world of home and society or as Knamiller (1987) concludes,

> School practice allows learning to remain rather separated from actual rural reality and it contains little in terms of skills or attitudes that enable school leavers to act innovatively in that environment.

Inevitably, calls for more relevance in curriculum content are heard, no less here than in developing contries. In 1987 I attended a UNESCO sponsored workshop in Botswana which attempted to rewrite the Primary and Junior Secondary science syllabus as a 10-year programme. Content had to be drawn from what rural and urban adults and children would *need*: relevance was the key criterion. The task proved very difficult. The tendency was for the old 'fact dominated' pattern to assert itself over the new one of relevance. Attempts to make science less 'content based' are resisted on the grounds that it must not lose its academic rigour and exams are a sure means of defending it. Where ill-prepared and unsupported teachers are left to choose contexts for the processes of science to be practised, the critics point out the loss of continuity, progression and coverage.

Looking at the world scene, the extremes of 'content' or 'process' curricula are being abandoned as the limitations of both, as well as the realities of what teachers can be expected to achieve, are gradually understood by curriculum planners. Whether a Core Curriculum with science in it, as part of a National Curriculum under central, Ministerial control with National Tests at regular intervals in a child's schooling, will add up to genuine science education remains to be seen. My experience of centralised systems elsewhere doesn't encourage me to think so.

And in any case, does it matter for the vast majority of the world's children whether they are able to carry out the processes and recite the knowledge? Few will be scientists or technologists or technicians. Though more and more will encounter the products, both beneficial and harmful, of science, like most of the present adults of our society, they will remain ignorant to a large extent of how or why, content to drive their vehicle, switch on their radio, swallow their medicine and eat their food. Are we crying for the moon when we primary teachers set out to make mini-scientists of a whole generation?

Chapter 10

Primary Science Teaching in a Developing Country: The Lesson we can Learn

Mwangi K Githui

Overview

The system of education operated in Kenya since 1963 is based on the three-tier model developed during the latter part of the colonial period, which in turn was influenced by the system of education in Britain. The administration and policy control of education in Kenya rests with the Minister for Education who is charged with the responsibility for promoting education of the people of Kenya. Education is therefore highly centralised, with a common curriculum, based on the 'centre–periphery' model and common national examinations at the end of each phase of the three-tier system.

In any society education has two major functions: introducing each new generation of students to society's culture and values, and imparting skills that will enable the youth to contribute to the society's economy. Both these functions are fundamental to a developing country like Kenya which, at one and the same time, is reasserting its pre-colonial identity and attempting to develop socially and economically into the modern world.

Since independence, our education system has been characterised by a rapid and massive expansion of schools at all levels, operating largely a literary-based curriculum and using traditional methods of teaching. Initially, this was a response to the acute shortage of professional and middle-level manpower created by the departure of expatriate staff after independence in 1963. The expansion occurred so rapidly, due to heavy government investment and public support for education, that it quickly reached and surpassed the capacity of the economy to provide the kind of occupations which school leavers had been led to expect.

Ten years after independence, as the country took stock of its progress, new concerns became apparent and new problems emerged, all of which brought into question the continued suitability of the existing pattern of education provision. Kenyan educationalists and the public at large became concerned with the massive wastage at the end of each educational cycle, especially at the primary school level.

In Kenya, the number of primary school pupils does not match the number of available places in the country's secondary schools. Consequently, during the final year of the primary school, the pupils have to sit a selection examination – the Kenya Certificate of Primary Education (KCPE) whose results determine who will proceed to secondary school.

The unfortunate fact is that of all 350,000 pupils who sit KCPE, only aproximately 30% eventually get a place in the secondary schools. This leaves the majority of children aged between 12 and 13 years feeling they have nowhere to go and not much to do.

Up to 1974, the type of education that primary leavers had gone through was diametrically opposed to the realities of life that they now had to face. All through their primary school life, they had been prepared for and hoped to start a secondary education, following an academic-oriented curriculum and eventually looking toward a white-collar job. Instead, they now had to go back to their rural community and environment totally unprepared for what lay in store. Their academic primary 'education' was of little use out there. They had no skills and no positive attitudes to help them solve the practical problems of everyday life that now surrounded them. They painfully realised that the facts and bits of information they had memorised passively in school were irrelevant, and in a year or so, the majority of these primary school leavers reverted to illiteracy.

This massive primary school drop-out with no useful skills, labelled the 'school-leaver problem', prompted an urgent review of the country's education policy and practice.

In addition there was now increasing concern about:

1   The attitude among the people that formal education automatically led to employment with high wages in the modern urbanised sector of the economy.
2   Expectations of school leavers that formal education qualified them for employment.
3   Education divorcing youth from their rural environment with consequent migration to urban areas.
4   The rapidity with which the school curriculum was becoming obsolete in the face of the very rapid economic social and political changes.
5   Inappropriate, ineffective teaching and learning methods relying on

rote learning and cramming to enable pupils to pass the numerous examinations they had to sit.

As Tony Russell has pointed out in Chapter 9, many of these concerns are shared by other African states. The government addressed itself to these key problems and set up several committees and commissions. They sought to evaluate all aspects of education and to make appropriate recommendations. The most prominent of these committees was the National Committee on Educational Objectives and Policies (NCEOP) of 1975. Among the recommendations made in its report (Republic of Kenya, 1976) were:

(a)   a radical change in the curriculum at all levels to make it more relevant to the country's current and future needs;
(b)   an improvement in the qualitative and quantitative aspects of teacher education.

The report advocated change from formal, didactic teaching methods to a wider use of active learning methods aimed at developing a child's potential to the full. Ultimately, this led to a revised curriculum embodying dynamic methods of teaching and learning.

The new curriculum at the primary school level was aimed at helping the majority of pupils for whom formal education is terminal at this level, to lead productive and useful lives as self-reliant individuals in their own local communities. Although the change affected all subjects, it had greatest impact in primary science.

The Kenya science curriculum before 1975

As noted in the Bessey Report of 1972 on curriculum in Kenya (Republic of Kenya, 1972), the science syllabus for the upper primary classes was too long and dwelt mainly on acquisition of scientific information and facts. The teachers, in an effort to cover and finish the syllabus, did little else except dish out masses of information and facts to a passive class with the hope that something would 'sink' into the pupils' heads. In turn the pupils were for most of the time busy listening to the teacher and copying lengthy notes from the chalkboard. These notes were later memorised with the hope that during the final examination pupils would be able to recall and reproduce whatever they had 'learnt' by rote to answer questions and pass.

The atmosphere in the classrooms of that period was tense. Desks and chairs were neatly arranged in rows that had to be equidistant to the millimetre. The teacher's table lay in front with a long cane at one end, which by its mere presence meant deadly silence. The pupils had to sit and listen. No activities were carried out at all and questions were to be asked only when the teacher invited the same. This was the 'learning situation'.

By the very nature of the science curriculum operating prior to 1975, a barrier had already been created between the home and school environment. Pupils in the tropics would be taught about plants and animals commonly found in spring, in the temperate lands, but not about what was around them. The teacher would tackle the topic on machines and motion by happily quoting examples such as the rack and pinion, helical double gears and so on, which were outside the pupils' experience, instead of investigating how pupils can make or improve the handcarts and wheelbarrows which they use to transport farm produce to the market.

Topics that would have a direct bearing on the pupils' lives or environment were not in the science syllabus. Topics such as environmental conservation, medicinal herbs, simple construction, soil erosion, improvisation of tools or community health problems related to science did not feature in the curriculum. Thus from the outset, education was for school and not for the pupil in his surroundings and community. Little wonder that the 70 per cent who did not secure places in the secondary schools would justifiably conclude that education was of little or no value to them.

New curriculum policy for science

Following the New Government Policy on Education in 1976 (Republic of Kenya, 1976) there was drastic change in the primary science curriculum, support materials (such as teachers' guides and radio programmes), the proposed teaching and learning approach, and examinations set at local and national level. Broad and specific objectives for primary science were drawn up in line with the new policy. To support this, new syllabuses were developed through the system of panels at the Kenya Institute of Education (KIE). KIE is the national centre for curriculum research and development where all curriculum and related materials below university level are prepared. Specifically, the 'knowledge' component that was characteristic of the old syllabuses was greatly reduced and replaced by topics that are more or less directly related to life themes and everyday problems in the pupils' local environment, such as our environment, transport, energy, conservation, improvisation of domestic equipment, and so on.

In addition the new syllabus had a heavy dose of experimental work and stressed the practical aspect at all levels, so that pupils could learn how to learn as they engaged in activities where they solved problems on their own. The new syllabus encouraged learning from the pupils' local environment by making visits to places of interest, doing project work on their own, and using locally available materials and improvisation in the making of apparatus for their experimental and general use.

Thus the new philosophy was to equip the primary school leavers with skills, attitudes and flexibility compatible with the kind of life that they would be likely to lead in the rural areas and with the practical problems that they definitely would encounter. In the new policy and curriculum, science was viewed and perceived as a medium through which a child might develop natural curiosity, powers of observation and enquiry, and constructive attitudes to problem-solving and decision making.

To the general public there was, now, a clear relationship between the school curriculum and the home environment, in that what the children learned in school was related to and relevant to their day-to-day lives.

Support materials

In the old syllabuses, a list of reference books that the teacher was required to consult were listed after each topic. Unfortunately, the contents of these reference books ended up word for word in the pupils' books as teachers lifted chunks from textbooks and copied them out for pupils.

For the new syllabus, a set of new books was issued, to be used in conjunction with some smaller units (booklets) for each topic. The *Guidelines for Teaching Science* (Kenya Ministry of Education, 1978) and the *Kenya Primary Science* (Berluti, 1981b) booklets had very little factual information in them. They comprised suggested activities and questions to be answered through group or individual investigations.

For instance, in the *Kenya Primary Science* booklet entitled *Ask the ant-lion* (Kenya Ministry of Education, 1976) one can quickly observe the teaching approach being advocated. As children observed ant-lions they asked the teacher a variety of questions.

- Where does the ant-lion live?
- What does it eat?
- Can the ant-lion dig in maize flour and chalk dust?

- What would happen if an insect larger than the ant-lion entered in the ant-lion's trap?
- How does the ant-lion catch its prey?

In the traditional classroom, the teacher would have answered these questions at once or referred the children to some textbook. In these booklets no answers are provided and the teacher is asked to throw every question back to the pupils and tell them 'ask the ant-lion, it has all the answers'. The teacher is then instructed to provide the necessary materials for the pupils, and guide them to answer their own questions.

Take-up of the new teaching–learning methods

Initially, this posed a difficult task for trainers, since human nature tends to be conservative; whenever there is 'change' only a few join the bandwagon for better or worse. Another small group sits by the fence to wait and see, while the majority quietly resist the change.

When the new curriculum was introduced, efforts were made to hold updating and in-service courses for teachers in schools and tutors in teacher training colleges. However, it was not possible to in-service every teacher at once in the republic. It was therefore left to those who had been in-serviced to go and organise in-service courses in their own schools and update their teacher colleagues accordingly, using a 'cascade' approach.

The new method was referred to by many names: the activity method, the enquiry approach, the learner-centred method and the discovery technique, among others. What was being stressed was a dynamic, investigatory aspect rather than a static, passive mode of learning.

It was a radical shift from the traditional method of teaching. And as Tony Russell has shown in Botswana, those teachers resisting adaptation to the new approach in Kenya also had their reasons. They felt that their authority in class had been eroded. Now there was far too much movement, activity and noise. The neat rows in the classroom were disrupted to give room to group work. The previously tidy classroom corners had now become junkyards full of materials collected for use by the pupils. There were too many haphazard outdoor activities during the science lessons. The traditional teacher was not sure of where he was treading. He felt he was losing class control and consequently his confidence. To him all this 'new' approach was the antithesis of learning and teaching.

It was this group of teachers who needed almost constant in-servicing, even coercion, through all available means. And the most formidable weapon, which teachers could not resist, was the National CPE Examination.

Change in the examinations

Prior to 1975/76, as already pointed out, the local and national examinations encouraged rote learning by consisting largely of items that tested the pupil's ability to memorise facts. It was realised that if the new curriculum were to achieve the desired effect, then all the examinations administered would have to change radically. The 'new examinations' backed up the 'objectives' and 'content' of the new curriculum and 'how' it was taught by now testing manual and thinking skills, positive scientific attitudes and a minimum of information.

Consequently, items found in the KCPE of 1976 awards had most items testing for pupils' ability to:

- design investigations
- identify problems
- control variables
- make accurate observations
- analyse information
- interpret results
- apply information
- make conclusions
- measure accurately

and so on. It was very clear that the new policy affecting curriculum change must be total, from the objectives through content and methodology to the assessment aspect. A loophole at any one stage could retard the whole system. It would have been a doubly futile effort if the pupils of those who taught the new approach were still tested on their ability to memorise facts only.

Let us look at a few items as they appeared in the final examination *before* and *after* the new science policy and curriculum came into effect.

Before the new curriculum, items such as these were common:

(i)   Which one of the following plants produces flowers?
A. Ferns B. Fungi C. Bananas D. Algae

(ii) If you hold a long pencil so that part of it is under water, it looks bent. The scientific name for the cause of this is:
A. diffusion B. dispersion C. refraction D. reflection

(iii) Houseflies are dangerous to our health because they can spread three of the following diseases. Which one of these diseases is not carried by houseflies?
A. Typhoid B. Cholera C. Sleeping sickness D. Dysentry

After 1975, with the introduction of the new curriculum the final science examinations were dominated by questions such as these:

(i)   As Komir was running from the house to the shop one evening, he noticed his shadow stretching away on his left. In which direction was he running?
A. North B. East C. West D. South

(ii) Substances which turn the juice from red hibisucs flowers green, are called bases. Substances which turn the hibiscus juice pink, are called acids. Ali tested different substances with the hibiscus juice and recorded his results in the following chart:

	lemon juice	solution of ashes	vinegar	milk	solution of soap
turns pink	yes	no	yes	no	no
turns green	no	yes	no	no	yes

Using the chart, which one of the following conclusions is CORRECT?
A.   Milk and soap solution are both acids
B.   Soap solution is a base and lemon juice is an acid
C.   Ashes solution and vinegar are both bases
D.   Vinegar is an acid and lemon juice is a base

(iii) The chart below shows a simple food web

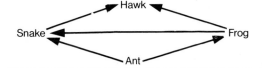

> What would be the immediate effect if all the snakes were killed?
> A. Hawks would increase and ants decrease
> B. Frogs would decrease and ants increase
> C. Frogs would increase and hawks increase
> D. Hawks would decrease and ants increase

The examiners, too, realised that much more was required of the primary school leaver than the mere ability to recall the facts memorised in school. Life after school demands that we be able to size up everyday situations, analyse the circumstances in which we find ourselves, apply our knowledge to seeing the options open to us in problem situations, and make judgements and decisions about what we should do in unfamiliar circumstances. These skills are particularly valuable for the majority of school leavers who will not receive any formal education after primary school.

With this in mind, the examiners' writing workshops put tremendous effort into generating an increasing range of items which tested investigative skills, and which were not biased in favour of urban children. For example, questions like this were deliberately included to descriminate in favour of rural and nomadic children, whose opportunity for close observation of natural phenomena was enchanced by their lifestyle.

3. Jane went to fetch water before sunrise, She saw the moon in the form of a thin crescent. Which of the following shapes of the moon did Jane see?

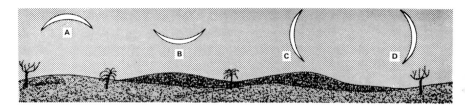

4. In which direction did Jane see the moon?
    A. North.   B. South.   C. East.   D. West.

This shift had a significant and positive influence on the teaching methods used in many schools, particularly where it was backed up by in-service sessions on the writing of such test items.

The new primary science syllabus (1976)

In this syllabus, which has now been revised over the years, the general aims of teaching science are expressed as follows:

1 That children acquire and preserve certain useful attitudes about themselves and their relationships with their environment.
2 That children acquire certain manual and thinking skills which are useful in solving practical problems.
3 That children acquire ways of seeking further knowledge and of using this knowledge to solve problems we meet in modern life.

But broad aims have to be translated into good classroom practices, and to assist teachers in doing so, the following steps were taken.

1 The objectives of good science teaching were identified at three levels in the primary school. Objectives were clearly spelt out for children in primary 1, 2 and 3 (6–8 years old); for children in primary 4 and 5 (9–10 years old) and for the 11–13-year-olds in primary 6, 7 and 8. Practising teachers and parents now had something to go by, a frame of reference as they taught or guided their children in science activities.
2 At each level, topic areas were suggested that could be used in teaching to achieve the stated objectives.
3 Over 50 Kenya Primary Science Units were written following the new policy. These contained detailed guidance as to how the objectives may be achieved through day to day teaching.

Teaching in the schools: the good, the not-so-good and the awful

With the introduction of the new primary science curriculum and activity methods of teaching, school inspectors and advisers had a busy schedule visiting schools to assess how the teachers were putting the new science policy into practice. As they went through a cross-section of classrooms in the countryside, they were able to discern various teaching and learning techniques employed by teachers.

The following account is taken from the experiences of a Mr Saitun, a school adviser who went visiting schools during the early stages of the implementation of the new policy and curriculum.

Mr Saitun went into a classroom in School 'A' in which the teacher was teaching the topic 'Fishes'. The teacher started by greeting the children, after which he demanded absolute silence. 'Fold your arms and listen to me carefully,' the teacher commanded. He then artistically drew the diagram of a fish on the chalkboard and labelled all the parts neatly. He then asked the children if they could all see his diagram on the chalkboard. They replied in a chorus, 'Yes, we can see it'. The teacher continued his lesson by writing the function of each part that he had labelled and asked children to read each function aloud, one by one. The children were then required to copy the teacher's notes. Upon completion of this exercise, the teacher turned to the class and asked the question 'What do the gills of a fish do?'. A row of hands went up and the teacher selected one pupil to answer. The pupil repeated with exactness what the teacher had written on the chalkboard. The teacher said 'That's very good'. . . . and the lesson ended.

Mr Saitun, who had sat and listened intently to what was going on in the classroom, made the following analysis of the lesson.

> The atmosphere of the class was quiet, almost tense. The pupils copied the teacher's notes but upon examination of some of their exercise books, errors in spelling were detected. The pupils were required to commit the information to memory.

After the lesson, Mr Saitun wondered, to what extent this lesson would contribute to the intelligent behaviour of each pupil in a new set of circumstances.

Mr Saitun later went to another classroom in school B where by some coincidence the topic being taught was also Fishes. In this class each group of four pupils was given a fish to observe, label, discuss and write down the function of each part. Further, each group was asked to compare the external features and functions of their specimen with those of other fish the teacher had brought into the classroom. The pupils worked mostly on their own with occasional assistance from the teacher. At the end of the lesson, the teacher asked the pupils to consider in what ways the external features of a fish help it to live successfully in water.

In analysing this lesson, Mr Saitun noted that the pupils were provided with actual specimens; they were required to relate information they gathered on their own to other kinds of fish and that to be able to answer the teacher's question, the pupils had to do more than recall the information which they had acquired. Mr Saitun concluded that some depth of understanding had been achieved and some learning had taken place.

Continuing with his visits, Mr Saitun went to yet another classroom in school C, where he found to his amazement that the teacher was teaching the same topic, Fishes. In this classroom the teacher started his lesson by posing the following problem: 'What enables fish to move in a straight line?'

The question by the teacher caused each pupil to make himself a part of a group that would work on different approaches to part of the project that interested him. One group was to construct an aquarium in which the fish would be kept. Another group was to make fishing nets, and a third was to go to the small school library to look up information on the problem. Each group organised how it would carry out its tasks and then the groups exchanged notes. Towards the end of the lesson, the groups got together and decided on a suitable time on a Saturday morning when they would all meet to go out to the nearby dam and catch fish.

A follow up of this lesson in the following week revealed that the pupils had caught several fish which they put in their aquarium. After careful observation of how the fishes were moving, and with the information gathered from the library, the pupils were able to suggest answers to the question given.

Mr Saitun concluded that in this class the pupils were doing a lot of thinking, were actively involved in doing the various tasks, and in so doing were acquiring some attitudes towards problem-solving, some skills and also some factual information.

If one now analyses the levels of interactions observed in the three classrooms, some general conclusions can be drawn.

1 In class A, the pupils were passively committing information to memory. But, given a different set of circumstances, the pupils could not have used the information.
2 In class B, the method used enabled the pupils to isolate units of information and see how these pieces fit together. It could be said, they understood something about what they were doing and a certain amount of learning was taking place.
3 In class C, the problem posed by the teacher set the whole class in motion and demanded that the pupils reflect on the problem.

In thinking about the problem, the children in class C utilised available sources of information, constructed equipment and collected specimens. From their observation of the fish, data were obtained, the analysis of which provided possible answers to their problem. As they made the aquarium and the fishing nets, and caught the fish, the pupils must have acquired numerous manual and mental skills which could be used in out-of-school settings. At this level, no doubt, meaningful learning took place.

Experiences in school A were the order of the day before the new policy came into effect. Practices in school B were fairly common during the transition period, and in C, the new policy in science teaching at its best is portrayed. For pupils to learn, they must actively participate in the learning process.

We should not imagine that all schools were of type C or ever would be. Nevertheless, those who frequently observed science being taught in primary schools in Kenya were aware that an increasing number of teachers were realising that pupils did better in the CPE examination when they taught according to model C, and a continuous shift towards this model was discernible.

The value of problem-solving through science

Let us now briefly examine how the teaching of science following the new and revised syllabus in two schools illustrates the value of science in tackling real problems and the skills children learn through this.

1. *Heat: Fire: Cooking*

After discussions on the topic of heat energy, the teacher came up with questions related to the type of fires the children make, and how cooking is done at their homes. A lot of domestic cooking in Kenya is done with charcoal braziers called 'jikos' which are made from metal drums. As pupils were investigating the various ways of cooking used in their homes, they decided to find out how efficient a jiko is and how they can make a better one.

In the ordinary jiko much of the heat produced by charcoal escapes from the sides and is lost through conduction and radiation. After trying several models and comparing their efficiencies, the children came up with an improved jiko which has a metal frame enclosing a thick layer of hardened clay. This new jiko was four times more efficient than the ordinary one in terms of saving fuel.

The children started making these improved jikos during their free time and in a few months time, the improved jiko became a common cooker in the local villages. During the District Agricultural Show, the children of this school displayed and 'demonstrated' the efficiency of their improved jiko to the public. They won a cash prize and a small trophy from the Ministry of Energy.

In another school, primary 7 pupils studying the topic of wind started off by making simple paper propellers and running around with them. As they explored the possible uses of wind, they decided to make simple

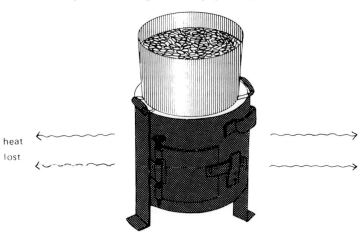

windmills using tin foil. They then fixed these windmills on the roof of their classroom. As they turned continuously, children were fascinated. From these simple windmills, the children embarked on a bigger project using junk collected from local garages and blacksmiths' yards, and gradually constructed a huge windmill formidable in the sense that as it turned and gathered speed, it shook the ground around it for up to 15 metres.

This windmill was then used in the school to cut wood, grind maize grains into flour and pump water. This project attracted a lot of visitors including officials from the Ministry of Education, all of whom were impressed by the impact made by the new science policy.

Pupils also improvised their own tools such as hammers using old nuts and bolts and these kinds of activity gradually found their way into the science schemes used to teach the new curriculum, as illustrated by the following example.

The shape of the tool is important:
• Why is the head flat?
(Suppose it was not.)
• Why is there a handle?
(Suppose there was no handle.)
The properties of the materials are important:
• Why is the head made of iron?
(What properties of iron make it better than wood?)
• Why is the handle made of wood?
(What properties of wood make it better than iron?)
• Which method of making a hammer do you think is the best, this one or the one you used in Standard 6?

Think of ways in which your hammer could be improved.
• Could it be made of better materials?
• Could its shape be better?
• Should its size be different?
• Does it alter while you are using it. For example:
— does the nut come loose?
— does the handle split?
Discuss your improvements. Draw designs. Collect new materials,
— better ones if possible.
• Can you make a better hammer than before?
• How can you find out if it is really better?

Thus, if we re-visit the school adviser's experiences in school C, we can see a clear correlation between the problem-solving approach to learning science and pupils' creativity, inventiveness and application of science and scientific skills to solve real practical problems in their local communities and environment.

New policies in curriculum implementation: discussion issues

From the Kenyan experience there are certain issues that crop up whenever changes in the existing policy and curriculum take place, which warrant further discussion. They relate to teachers, pupils, schools, examinations and the real community.

Teachers

- Teacher attitudes to change may spell success or doom to a new innovation. What attitudes are teachers taking?
- Due to early specialisation by teachers before qualifying as teachers, some of them may not feel competent to handle science teaching as required. What can be done?
- It is not possible to update all teachers adequately as soon as an innovation is introduced. What are priorities?
- The presence of a large number of unqualified teachers in the primary schools (in Kenya nearly 30% of all primary school teachers are not trained). What training is needed?

Pupils

- Some cultural backgrounds and practices may present barriers to learning certain aspects of science. How can they be overcome?
- Language is often a barrier since the medium of instruction could be a second or third language. In Kenya, from primary 4 onwards (age 9) the medium of instruction is English – a third language. How do we minimise the adverse effects of this, particularly in assessing and examining?

Schools

- There are wide variations in physical facilities, which in some cases are found wanting and not conducive to sound science learning practices. Whose responsibility is it to eradicate this disadvantage?

Centralised curriculum

- In a land of contrasts ranging from the coast to a snow-capped mountain on the equator, using a common syllabus and activities brings problems of its own. How do we encourage local variation within the context of a National Examination?

Examinations

- The terminal primary school examination is still selective. As such the tendency to drill pupils in what is perceived as the likely questions still persists, and takes a lot of contact time especially in the final year of primary school. What will dissuade teachers from this approach?

Local community

- The enthusiasm and support that the school gets from the local parents can enhance or retard the implementation of a new policy. How can this be fostered?

References

ALBURY, D. and SCHWARZ, J. (1982) *Partial Progress: The Politics of Science and Techology* (London: Pluto Press).

ASSOCIATION FOR SCIENCE EDUCATION (1981) *Education through Science: Policy Statement* (ASE).

ASSOCIATION FOR SCIENCE EDUCATION (1986) *Science Teachers' Handbook* (London: Hutchinson).

BACCHUS, M.K. (1981) 'Education for development in underdeveloped countries', *Comparative Education*, 17 (2), 215–227.

BAEZ, A.V. (1976) *Innovation in Science Education World Wide* (Paris: UNESCO).

BARNES, N. and EDGE, D. (1982) *Science in Context* (Milton Keynes: Open University Press).

BARON, S. (1988) 'Community and the limits of democracy: scene from the politics' in GREEN, A. and BALL, S. (eds) *Progress and Inequality in Comprehensive Education* (London: Routledge) pp.82–101.

BATESON, P. and SHEPHERD, T. (1988) *The Water Game: A Topic-based Computer Simulation* (London: Centre for World Development Education).

BERLUTI, A. (1981a) *Beginning Science: A Course for Primary Schools in Kenya* (London: Macmillan Kenya).

BERLUTI, A. (1981b) *C.P.E. Science* (Nairobi: Macmillan Kenya).

BERLUTI, A. (1985) *Beginning Science (Standard 8)* (Nairobi: Macmillan Kenya).

BHATTACHARYA, S. and RAMACHANDRAN, K. (1987) *Exploring Environment – Science Books 1–3* (New Delhi: National Council for Educational Research and Training).

BIRD, J. and DIAMOND, D. (1975) *Candles*, Teaching Primary Science Series (Hemel Hempstead: Macdonald Educational).

BIRMINGHAM DEVELOPMENT EDUCATION CENTRE (1986) *A Sense of School: active learning approach to INSET in development education in the primary school* (Birmingham DEC).

BRITISH BROADCASTING CORPORATION (1988) *Instruments of the World* (BBC Enterprises).

BROOKING, C., FOSTER, M. and SMITH, S. (1981) *Teaching for Equality: Educational Resources on Race and Gender* (Runnymede Trust).

BUTTON, J. (1989) *The Primary School in a Changing World: A Handbook for Teachers* (London: CWDE).

CARRINGTON, B. and TROYNA, B. (1988) 'Combating racism through political education', in CARRINGTON, B. and TROYNA, B. (eds) *Children and Controversial Issues: Strategies for the Early and Middle Years of Schooling* (London: The Falmer Press) pp. 205–222.

CASTLE, E.B.(1972) *Education for Self-Help: New Strategies for Developing Countries* (Oxford: Oxford University Press).

DEPARTMENT OF EDUCATION AND SCIENCE (1978) *Primary Education in England: A Survey by H.M. Inspectors of Schools* (HMSO).

DEPARTMENT OF EDUCATION AND SCIENCE (1985a) *Education for All* (The Swann Report) Cmmd. 9453 (HMSO).

DEPARTMENT OF EDUCATION AND SCIENCE (1985b) *Science 5–16: A Statement of policy* (HMSO).

DEPARTMENT OF EDUCATION AND SCIENCE (1985c) *Better Schools* Cmnd. 9469 (HMSO).

DEPARTMENT OF EDUCATION AND SCIENCE (1987) *The National Curriculum 5–16: A Consultation Document* (DES).

DEPARTMENT OF EDUCATION AND SCIENCE (1988a) *Science for Ages 5–16* (DES).

DEPARTMENT OF EDUCATION AND SCIENCE (1988b) *The Development Programme for Race Equality in the London Borough of Brent: Report by H.M. Inspectors* (DES).

DEPARTMENT OF EDUCATION AND SCIENCE (1989a) *National Curriculum: From Policy to Practice* (DES).

DEPARTMENT OF EDUCATION AND SCIENCE (1989b) *Responses to Ethnic Diversity in Teacher Training* (DES).

DEPARTMENT OF EDUCATION AND SCIENCE (1989c) *Science in the National Curriculum* (HMSO).

DITCHFIELD, C. (ed)/SSCR (1987) *Better Science: Working for a Multicultural Society* (ASE/Heinemann for SSCR).

DOUGLAS, O., WALKER, E. and AGARDE, K. (1988) *Science Revision and Tests for the Caribbean* (Basingstoke: Macmillan Caribbean).

DRIVER, R. (1981) 'Pupils' alternative frameworks in science' *European Journal of Science Education*, 3 (1), 93–101.

DRIVER, R. (1983) *The Pupil as Scientist?* (Milton Keynes: Open University Press).

DRIVER, R., GUESNE, E. and TIBERGHIEN, A. (1985) *Childrens Ideas in Science* (Milton Keynes: Open University Press).

DUROJAIYE, M.O.A. (1980) *The Contribution of African Universities to the Reform of Education* (Paris: UNESCO).

ELKIN, J. and TRIGGS, P. (1985) *Childrens Books for a Multicultural Society,*

(London: Books for Keeps).

FISHER, S. and HICKS, D. (1985) *World Studies 8-13* (Edinburgh: Oliver and Boyd).

GILL, D. and LEVIDOW, L. (1987) *Anti-Racist Science Teaching* (London: Free Association Press).

HARLEN, W. (1982) Report of the Seminar on Primary Science, Bandung, Indonesia (mimeo).

HATCHER, R. (1987) 'Race and Education: Two perspectives for change' in TROYNA, B. (ed) *Racial Inequality in Education* (London: Tavistock) pp. 184–200.

HAWES, H. (1979) *Curriculum and Reality in African Primary Schools* (Longman).

ILEA SCIENCE CENTRE (1987) *Science Teaching in a Multicultural Society. Book 1: Suggestions and Resources, Book 2: Issues Practices and Resources* (ILEA).

INGLE, R.B. and TURNER, A.D. (1981) 'Science curricula as cultural misfits', *European Journal of Science Education*, 3 (4), 357–371.

INSTITUTE OF RACE RELATIONS (1982) *Roots of Racism*.

JACKSON, P. (1968) *Life in Classrooms* (Holt, Rinehart and Winston).

JAHODA, G. (1970) 'Supernatural beliefs and changing cognitive structures among Ghanaian university students', *Journal of Cross-Cultural Psychology*, 1 (2), 115–130.

JEFFS, T. (1988) 'Preparing young people for participatory democracy' in CARRINGTON, B. and TROYNA , B. (eds) *Children and Controversial Issues: Strategies for the Early and Middle Years of Schooling* (London: The Falmer Press) pp.29–53.

JONES, L. (1985) *Science and the Seeds of History* (Birley High School/Manchester Ed.Dept).

KELLY, A. *et al*, (1985) 'Traditionalists and trendies: teachers' attitudes to educational issues', *British Educational Research Journal*, 11 (2), 91–104.

KELLY, G.A. (1955) *The Psychology of Personal Constructs*, Vols.1 and 2, (New York: Norton and Company).

KENYA MINISTRY OF EDUCATION (1976) *Ask the ant-lion* (Kenya Primary Science Units) (Nairobi: Jomo Kenyatta Foundation).

KENYA MINISTRY OF EDUCATION (1978) *Guidelines for Teaching Science: Standard 7 Teachers' Guide* (Nairobi: Jomo Kenyatta Foundation).

KERR, J. and ENGEL, E. (1980) 'Should Science be taught in primary schools?', *Education 3-13*, 8 (1), 4–8.

KLEIN, G. (1984) 'Criteria for selecting classroom materials', in *Resources for Multicultural Education* (Schools Council Publications/SCDC).

KNAMILLER, G.W., BAEZ, A.V. and SMYTH, J.C. (eds) (1987) *The Environment and science and technology education* (Oxford: Pergamon).

KUHN, T.S. (1962) *The Structure of Scientific Revolutions* (Chicago: University of Chicago Press).

LAKATOS, I. (1970) 'Falsification and the methodology of scientific research programmes', in LAKATOS, I. and MUSGRAVE, A. (eds) *Criticism and the Growth of Knowledge* (Cambridge: Cambridge University Press).

LAYTON, D.(1984) *Interpreters of Science* (London: John Murray/ASE).

LEICESTERSHIRE LEA (1987) *An Aide Memoire for Multicultural Education* (Leicestershire Centre for Multicultural Education).

LINDSAY, L. (1985) *Racism, Science Education and the Politics of Food* (London: ALTARF).

LYNCH, J. (1987) *Prejudice Reduction and the Schools* (London: Cassell).

MANN, J., PEACOCK, A. and TOWNEND, C. (1988), 'Teaching science multiculturally in primary schools: recent initiatives in Leicestershire', *Leicestershire Education* No.9, pp.12–15.

MULLARD, C. (1986) *Pluralism, Ethnicism and Ideology: Implications for a Transformative Pedagogy* (Centre for Race and Ethnic Studies, University of Amsterdam, Working Paper No.2).

NATIONAL CURRICULUM SCIENCE WORKING GROUP (1987) *Interim Report* (DES).

NATIONAL CURRICULUM TASK GROUP ON ASSESSMENT AND TESTING (TGAT) (1987) *A Report* (DES).

NOTT, M. and WATTS, D.M. (1987) 'Towards a multicultural and anti-racist science education policy', *Education in Science* Vol.121 (January).

OLDMAN, D. (1987) 'Plain speaking and pseudo-science: the "New Right" attack on anti-racism', in TROYNA, B. (ed) *Racial Inequality in Education* (Tavistock) pp.29–43.

ORTONY, A. (1975) 'Why metaphors are necessary and not just nice', *Education Theory*, 25, 45–53.

OSBORNE, J., BLACK, P., SMITH, M. and MEADOWS, J. (1990) *Light (SPACE Projects Report)* (Liverpool University Press).

OSBORNE, R. (1983), *Learning in Science Project*, Working Paper No.115 (Waikato University, New Zealand).

OSBORNE, R. and FREYBERG, P. (1985) *Learning in Science* (London: Heinemann).

OTAALA, B. (1981) 'Programme on concept development in African children', in OTAALA, B. and PANDEY, S. (eds) (1981) *Educational Research in Boleswa Countries* (Gaborone: University of Botswana).

OVERSEAS DEVELOPMENT ADMINISTRATION (1982) *Annual Report* (O.D.A.).

OXFAM (1987) *The World in a Supermarket Bag* (Oxfam).

PAREKH, B. (1986) 'The concept of multicultural education', in MOGDIL,

S., VERMA, G., MALLICK, K. and MOGDIL, C. (eds) *Multicultural Education, the Interminable Debate* (London: The Falmer Press) pp.19–32.

PEACOCK, A. (1986) *Science Skills: A Problem-Solving Activities Book* (London: Macmillan Education).

PEACOCK, A. (1989) 'What parents think about science in primary schools', *Primary Science Review*, No.10.

PLIMMER, D. (1981) 'Science in the primary schools: what went wrong?' *The School Science Review*, 62, 641–647.

POPE, M.L. and WATTS, D.M. (1988) 'Constructivist goggles: implications for process in teaching and learning physics', *European Journal of Physics*, No.9, 101–109.

PRATT, J. (1985) 'The attitudes of teachers', in WHYTE, J., DEEM, R, KANT, L. and CRUIKSHANK, M. (eds) (1985) *Girl-Friendly Schooling* (London: Methuen) pp.24–35.

PRESTT, B. (1988) 'Science in the primary school', *Education in Science*, 127, 11–12.

RENNIE, J. (ed.) (1985) *British Community Primary Schools: Four Case Studies* (London: The Falmer Press).

REPUBLIC OF KENYA (1972) *Kenya Curriculum Commission: the Bessey Report* (Nairobi: Government Printer).

REPUBLIC OF KENYA (1976) *National Committee on Educational Objectives and Policies* (Nairobi: Government Printer).

ROSS, A. (1984) 'Developing political concepts and skills in the primary school', *Educational Review*, 36 (2), 131–139.

RUSSELL, T. and WATT, D. (1990a) *Evaporation and Condensation* (SPACE Project) (Liverpool University Press).

RUSSELL, T. and WATT, D. (1990b) *Growth* (SPACE Project) (Liverpool University Press).

SCHOOLS COUNCIL (1979) *Impact and Take-up Project* (Schools Council/Longman).

SCHRODINGER, C. (1966) 'Is science a fashion of the times?', in VAVOULIS, A. and COLVER, A.W. (eds) *Science and Society: Selected Essays* (San Franscisco: Holden-Day).

SCIENCE FOR A MULTICULTURAL SOCIETY GROUP (1985) *Science Education for a Multicultural Society* (Leicestershire LEA).

SCIENCE PROCESSES AND CONCEPT EXPLORATION (SPACE) PROJECT (1990) *See* Osborne *et al.*, 1990; Russell and Watt, 1990 a, b; Watt and Russell, 1990.

SECONDARY SCIENCE CURRICULUM REVIEW (1983) *Science Education 11–16: Proposals for Action and Consultation* (SSCR).

SERTIMA, I. (1984) *Blacks in Science, Ancient and Modern* (Transaction Books USA).

SIFUNA, D. (1974) 'Some factors affecting the quality of teaching in primary schools in Kenya', *Education in Eastern Africa*, 4 (2).

SMART, N.D.J. (1981), 'Teachers, teacher education and the community', in GARDNER, R. (ed.) *Teacher education in Developing Countries: Prospects for the Eighties* (London: University of London Press).

SNOW, C.P. (1959) *The Two Cultures* (Cambridge: Cambridge University Press).

SOLOMON, J. (1983) *How can we be sure? Science in a social context*. (Oxford: Blackwell).

STENHOUSE, D. (1985) *Active Philosophy in Education and Science: Paradigms and Language Games* (London: George Allen and Unwin).

STEPANS, J. (1986) 'Misconceptions die hard' *Science Teacher*, 53 (6), 65–69.

STOLLAR, H. (1985) *Water Technology from Around the World* (Waltham Forest Teachers Centre).

TOULMIN, S.E. (1961) *Foresight and Understanding* (London: Hutchinson).

TROYNA, B. (1984) 'Multicultural Education: emancipation or containment?', in BARTON, L. and WALKER, S. (eds) *Social Crisis and Educational Research* (London: Croom Helm) pp.75–97.

TROYNA, B. (1987) 'Beyond Multiculturalism: towards the enactment of antiracist education in policy provision and pedagogy', *Oxford Review of Education*, 13 (3), 307–320.

TROYNA, B. and BALL, W. (1987) *Views from the Chalk Face: School Responses to an LEA's Policy on Multicultural Education* (2nd edn) (Centre for Research in Ethnic Relations, University of Warwick, Policy Paper 1).

TURNER, S. and TURNER, T. (1987) 'Multicultural education in the initial training of science teachers', *Research in Science and Technological Education*, 5 (1), 25–36.

UNESCO (1980) *Final Report of the Meeting of Experts on the Incorporation of Science and Technology into the Primary School Curriculum* (Paris: UNESCO).

VANCE, M. (1987) 'Biology teaching in a racist society', in GILL, D. and LEVIDOW, L. *Anti-Racist Science Teaching* (London: Free Association Press).

WATT, D. and RUSSELL, T. (1990) *Sound* (SPACE Project) (Liverpool University Press).

WATTS, S. (1983) 'Science education for a multicultural society', *Multicultural Teaching*, 1 (3),3.

WHITE, P. (1983) *Beyond Domination: An Essay in the Political Philosophy of Education* (London: Routledge).

WILLIAMS, I. W. (1984) *Third World Science: Resource Materials for Science Teachers* (University College, Bangor).

WILLIAMS, M. (1986) 'The Thatcher generation', *New Society* (21 February 1986) pp.312–315.

WILLIAMS, R. (1987) *Children and World Development* (UNICEF UK/Richmond Publishing).

YOUNG, B.L. (1979) *Teaching Primary Science* (Longman (Nigeria)).

Science in Primary Schools: The Multicultural Dimension

Edited by

Alan Peacock

ROUTLEDGE

First published 1991 by Macmillan Education Ltd

Reprinted 1992
by Routledge
11 New Fetter Lane, London EC4P 4EE

Printed and bound in Hong Kong by
Astros Printing Ltd.

British Library Cataloguing-in-Publication Data

A catalogue record for this book is available from the British Library.

ISBN 0-415-09065-2